MATTHEW WEST

A DEVOTIONAL

HARVEST HOUSE PUBLISHERS
EUGENE, OREGON

Cover by Dual Identity, Inc.

Cover photo © James Steidl / Shutterstock

Published in association with the literary agency of The FEDD Agency, Inc., PO Box 341973, Austin, TX 78734.

TODAY IS DAY ONE

Copyright © 2015 Matthew West
Published by Harvest House Publishers
Eugene, Oregon 97402
www.harvesthousepublishers.com

ISBN 978-0-7369-4444-1 (hardcover)
ISBN 978-0-7369-4445-8 (eBook)

Printed in the United States of America

17 18 19 20 21 22 23 / ML-JH / 10 9 8 7 6 5 4

*This book is dedicated to all the people
who have shared their stories with me
over the past several years.*

*I have been inspired by witnessing how
God is at work in the lives of so many,
and I hope this book will be a daily reminder
that His redeeming work in our lives
is far from over.*

Acknowledgments

I want to thank my wife, Emily, and my two daughters, Luella and Delaney. Thank you for putting up with all the times you've asked me questions and I didn't answer because I was writing this book. Now, what was it you needed me to do? I'm all yours!

I also want to thank Nick Harrison and the team at Harvest House Publishers for your contribution to this book and your belief in me.

The steadfast love of the LORD never ceases;
his mercies never come to an end;
they are new every morning;
great is your faithfulness.

LAMENTATIONS 3:22-23

Contents

Introduction

The phone rang in the back room of a tiny pizza restaurant in the tiny town of Worthington, Minnesota.

"Thank you for calling Pizza Ranch," the young man answered. "How can I help you?"

"May I please speak to the manager?" I asked.

"Sure, hold on just a minute." The employee turned from the receiver and shouted, "Josh, it's for you!"

At first, I pretended I was calling to complain about my pizza, but then I told him the real reason for my call. "Josh, this is Matthew West. A while back you wrote your testimony and sent it to my website. Do you remember that?"

I could tell Josh was a little stunned when he answered, "Are you punking me?"

I laughed and told him that this was not a prank and that I was calling to tell him I had read his story.

He responded, "Oh, man, this is unbelievable! I think I need to sit down so I don't faint."

The story Josh sent me told of his difficult childhood. He grew up in the roughest area of a small town. The son of a single parent, he never met his mother. In his early teen years he got heavily involved in drugs, which soon turned to drug dealing...and trouble. At age 16, Josh's story took a drastic and devastating turn when he was arrested and sentenced to ten years in prison. From juvenile incarceration all the way to maximum-security prison, the next decade of his life had been laid out for him with the judge's verdict. In his letter to me, he wrote that he initially engaged in the typical prison lifestyle and did what he needed to do to survive. But then he began to feel that there was something more that his life could be, somebody new that he could become.

Behind bars, Josh began a personal relationship with Jesus, and his faith grew with every passing day. When someone gets "saved" in prison, other inmates often refer to that as "jailhouse religion"—a term intended to mean that a rock-bottom conversion wouldn't last once someone like Josh was released from prison and reintroduced to the free world. But after serving his ten years, Josh walked out of that prison determined to prove to himself and everyone else that he was indeed a changed man. He began applying for jobs...and that's when discouragement set in. No one was willing to take a chance on an ex-convict with tattoos on his knuckles and a troubled past.

Still, Josh kept the faith and got involved in a local church that continued to encourage him. A married couple from the church heard that Josh was in need of a helping hand and a new start. They operated a pizza restaurant and decided to take a chance on Josh, giving him a part-time job working in the back. What Josh wrote to me next was a beautiful illustration of how a second chance and the determination to change can turn a life around: "Matthew, I took that part-time job and ran with it. I worked my way up, and now I'm the manager of the Pizza Ranch in my hometown. If God can turn my life around, he can turn anyone's life around."

Josh's story is a powerful reminder that it's never too late to change your life. Of course, there are some things we can't change. No one can erase the past. As much as we wish there was a do-over, we all know there isn't. But we do have a daily chance to start over.

We read in Lamentations 3:23, "The steadfast love of the Lord never ceases; his mercies never come to an end; they are new every morning." That verse gives me fresh hope every morning. And I find myself in need of a daily reminder that God isn't done with me—that there's hope for this fresh, new day. I have a feeling I'm not the only one who feels that way. I bet you do too. In fact, I wrote this book in the hope that it might help to provide just that—a daily reminder that God's mercies are new every morning.

The best way to combat our tendencies to beat ourselves up for being less than perfect is to daily fill our hearts and minds with the truth and the hope of God's Word, which reminds us how deeply and endlessly we are loved by our Creator regardless of where we've been, what we've done, or how many times we've fallen short of perfection.

Meanwhile, back at the Pizza Ranch, my conversation with Josh continued. "Josh, have you by chance heard my new song 'Day One' on the radio lately?"

"Oh yeah, man! I actually told my wife when I heard it for the first time that I felt those lyrics were written just for me!" he said.

"Well, Josh," I said, "those lyrics *were* written for you. That's why I'm calling—to let you know that your testimony inspired me to write that song."

Josh got quiet for a few seconds, so I spoke up again. "Are you okay? You didn't drop a pizza, did you?"

We laughed, and then I heard him say, "I'm just blown away. Thank you so much! I just want my story to help people know they can change too."

For Josh, a new beginning in life came in the shape of a pizza. He went from being known as a drug addict and a lost cause in that small town of Worthington, Minnesota, to being the manager of a restaurant. His hometown newspaper even printed an article about a hometown boy making good.

What could a new beginning look like for you? Your today can be different from yesterday. And your tomorrow can be better than today. It's time to start over, starting now.

Today is Day One.

Be an Original, Not an Imitation

You, O Lord, are my hope,
my trust, O LORD, from my youth.
PSALM 71:5

Sometimes after a concert someone will tell me they envy me. They wish God would use them the same way He uses me. I'm glad people have dreams of being used by God. The problem is, when they have it all figured out how God should use them, they're boxing God in. God doesn't use everybody the same way.

With their focus on me or Jeremy Camp or Casting Crowns or Mandisa, they don't have eyes to see God's unique place for them. And they do have a place. *You* have a place. God won't allow any life that's surrendered to Him to go to waste. Just the opposite. When you're truly surrendered, God pours into you the abilities you need to walk out His will for the rest of your life. But it's one day at a time. One step forward into God's will every new morning.

Here's my advice to people who want to be used by God: Pray, wait, do the next thing you know to do, and trust God to open doors. The one thing *not* to do is to compare your usefulness to others. Don't settle for becoming just the next Billy Graham, Beth Moore, or Matthew West. God has a much better plan for you. By trusting Him on each Day One, you'll be moving one step closer to His plan.

Pray today, do what you know to do today, and leave the rest to God. Then repeat that formula again on tomorrow's new day. You will move yourself day by day into God's plan for you.

Are We There Yet?

Wait for the LORD;
be strong, and let your heart take courage;
wait for the LORD!

PSALM 27:14

"Are we there yet?" I'm pretty sure that's one of the oldest and most frequently asked questions in history. Can you picture the early settlers traveling by covered wagon in the 1800s? I'm sure plenty of kids were in the back of those wagons whining, "Are we there yet?"

Fast-forward from wagons on the Oregon Trail to minivans on the interstate. It still takes only a grand total of 30 seconds before I hear that same question shouted from the backseat—"Dad, are we there yet?"

Truthfully, this question isn't exclusive to the children. I've asked God the same question many times in my own journey of faith. I'm always waiting for that breakthrough. I'm waiting to see God do a miracle in my life. I'm waiting for my prayer to be answered. I'm waiting to see His plan for my life become a reality.

I'm anxious to arrive at my destination, and I don't enjoy feeling like a kid in the backseat of a minivan. My impatience often tempts me to hop in the front seat, take control of the wheel, and will my way to where I want to be—as if I knew better than God where I should be and when I should arrive. Yet when I turn to Scripture, I'm reminded that God's timing is perfect.

Sometimes strength means being able *not* to take control, but to wait on the Lord and trust that He will come through. And He will.

Today Is **DAY ONE**

Drop the Potatoes

Bear with each other and forgive one another if
any of you has a grievance against someone.
Forgive as the Lord forgave you.

COLOSSIANS 3:13 NIV

What do you do when someone says something that hurts? Do you
carry it around like a sack of potatoes day after day, week after
week? Sometimes when we do that, the sack gets heavier with each passing day.

God's way to deal with that sort of pain is to lay it down. That's it. Just
lay the thing down. "But that's hard," you say. Yeah, sometimes it's hard,
but remember this:

- It's harder to keep on carrying it. The difficulty in laying it
  down is momentary.
- Carrying the weight of your hurt will accomplish nothing.
- Nursing a grudge can become an addiction. You get used to
  the feeling of resentment and miss it when it's not there.
- If you're willing to carry one sack of potatoes, the enemy will
  eventually load you down with another sack. You develop
  the bad habit of taking offense when no offense was intended.
  The more sacks you carry, the slower you travel toward God's
  will.

Do you have a hurt you haven't let go of yet? Don't wait another day.
Drop the sack of potatoes on this Day One.

Today Is
**DAY
ONE**

Be Bold

Have I not commanded you? Be strong and courageous.
Do not be afraid; do not be discouraged, for the
LORD your God will be with you wherever you go.
JOSHUA 1:9 NIV

Do something bold and courageous today. And by bold and courageous, I don't mean you should sign up for a chili dog eating contest—I would actually advise against that. (And don't ask me how I know!)

I'm talking about being bold and courageous for Christ. God is calling you to big things. Perhaps that big thing popped into your head just as you read that last sentence. Or maybe you've sensed God calling you to something big, but you just aren't sure yet what that is. Sometimes we do know what big thing God is calling us to, but fear creeps up inside us and prevents us from stepping out in faith. Fear comes against us and asks, *What if I try and fail? What if I'm not really hearing from the Lord? What if it doesn't work out?*

It is not your job today to concern yourself with whether God's plan is going to work out. You are simply called to step out in faith.

In Joshua 1:9, the command "Do not be afraid" is followed by the reason why we don't have to fear: "God will be with you."

As you talk to God today, listen for His leading. Ask Him to show you the big plans He has for you. Then cast aside the fear and do something bold and courageous, knowing that God will be with you wherever you go.

Today Is DAY ONE

No Condemnation

I have the desire to do what is good, but I cannot carry it out. For I do not do the good I want to do, but the evil I do not want to do—this I keep on doing.

ROMANS 7:18-19 NIV

You blew it again, didn't you? You did, said, or thought something you said you never would again. And this isn't the first time. In fact, you've fallen into this trap many, many times. You vow not to let your mind go there, and within five minutes (or less!), off it goes. Wrong thoughts, wrong actions, wrong words—they'll get you every time.

Hey, you're not alone. Even the apostle Paul knew what it was like to want to do right and not be able to do it. That's clear from Romans 7—a chapter that could be the autobiography of just about any Christian.

The problem is, some Christians get stuck in Romans 7. They don't keep reading...

> There is therefore now no condemnation for those who are in Christ Jesus. For the law of the Spirit of life has set you free in Christ Jesus from the law of sin and death. (Romans 8:1-2 NIV).

If you're a believer in Christ, you have been placed "in Christ Jesus" and have the power to be free from the condemning cycle of sin and death.

Day One should always include a fresh realization that in Christ there is *no* condemnation. And there *is* power over sin. That's a great fact that will energize any new day.

Today Is DAY ONE

Be Still

Cease striving and know that I am God.
PSALM 46:10 NASB

Several years ago I faced a trial that God used to teach me a powerful lesson about being still. I lost my voice. I'm a singer and a songwriter, so that's pretty much the worst thing that could happen. I was forced to have surgery on my vocal chords and then spend two months in total silence while my voice healed—with no guarantees that I'd ever be able to sing again.

I soon discovered that my inability to speak increased my ability to listen. The words from Psalm 46:10 (NASB) came to life for me in a whole new way: "Cease striving and know that I am God."

In that season of my life, my season of silence, I was forced to cease striving for success or any other endeavors in my life. As a result, my heart began striving after God like never before. I wanted to be in His presence. I wanted to pray. I wanted to listen for His voice.

God taught me a powerful lesson during that season—there was nothing I could do in my own power to change my circumstances. And I experienced the power waiting to be discovered when I stopped long enough to listen and allow God to show me how great He is. I challenge you to be still today. Cease striving and be reminded that He is God and He is in control.

Satisfied

Satisfy us in the morning with your steadfast love,
that we may rejoice and be glad all our days.

Psalm 90:14

You know the feeling when you get up from a meal that was so great, you feel totally satisfied? That's the way getting up from a time of prayer can be. We can stand up from our knees feeling satisfied in having met with God.

Why? Because God created in us a hunger that only He can satisfy. We're made for Him, just as our stomachs are made for food. The great thing is that God delights in satisfying our hunger for Him. He delights in seeing us feed on Him day after day.

Just as our stomachs need to be satisfied with food every single day, so too our spirits need to be fed daily. In Psalm 90, the writer asks God, "Satisfy us in the morning," thus ensuring the rest of the day will find us rejoicing. Morning is a great time to be satisfied in the Lord, but we can come anytime and feast on Him. Sometimes before I go to bed, I find a rich time of fellowship with God. Whatever time works best for you, be sure your Day One always includes a time of satisfying yourself with the Lord.

Best Day Ever

He lifted me out of the pit of despair,
out of the mud and the mire.
He set my feet on solid ground
and steadied me as I walked along.

PSALM 40:2 NLT

A while back I was on a walk with my daughter Lulu. She ran up ahead of me and shouted at the top of her lungs, "BEST DAY EVER!"

I ran to catch up and asked her why this was the best day ever.

She replied, "I just saw a puppy!"

That's how it always is with my kids. Ice cream cone? BEST DAY EVER! Trip to Toys"R"Us? BEST DAY EVER! Afternoon at the pool? BEST DAY EVER!

It makes me wonder, *What was my best day ever?* Was it the day I graduated from college? My mom says that's the greatest miracle she's ever seen, but it's not my best day ever.

My wedding day? That was an awesome day—definitely right up there near the top of the list. But the best day ever in each of our lives is the day we decide to ask Jesus into our hearts—Day One of our spiritual journey.

So what's your best day ever? Take a moment to try and remember the hour you first believed in Christ. My dad always used to tell me that the day you say yes to Jesus is a memory you should always hold in your heart, just as you keep a picture in your wallet. Take that picture, keep it close to you, and remember that as your ultimate Day One.

Feeling His Pleasure

May the God of hope fill you with all joy and
peace in believing, so that by the power of the
Holy Spirit you may abound in hope.

Romans 15:13

Do you ever get restless? Maybe you wake up in the morning with a sense of uneasiness and you don't know why. Or maybe it comes over you in the evening. You come home and you're tired, but there's a sense that you've left something undone or that you want to be doing something...but what?

When that happens to me, sometimes it means another song is wanting to be written. God has called me to music, so there's a certain restlessness about not thinking musically each day.

For me it's music, and there's probably something like that for you. Writing? Preaching? Teaching? Loving on kids? Even sports can be that way. Did you ever see the movie *Chariots of Fire*? It's about Eric Liddell, an Olympic runner and missionary to China. He said, "I believe God made me for a purpose, but He also made me fast. And when I run, I feel His pleasure."

I feel His pleasure in music. Where do you feel His pleasure? Go there today.

What's on Your Name Tag?

See what great love the Father has lavished on us, that we should be called children of God! And that is what we are!

1 John 3:1 NIV

A young man named Jordan wrote me his story. The first sentence said, "Hello, my name is Jordan, and I am a drug addict." He went on to tell me he went from being an All-American college athlete to a college dropout and drug addict. But did Jordan quit when he hit rock bottom? No! He decided to fight. He spent a year at a Christian recovery program and graduated with a renewed commitment to Christ and a rediscovered identity in Christ. He went back to college and graduated with a master's degree. Today Jordan is married, he's a high school teacher and basketball coach, and even better, God has called him into ministry.

Remember today that you're not defined by your successes or by your failures. Consider 1 John 3:1. Aren't you glad that verse wasn't written in the past tense? "And that is what you *were* before you went and screwed it up, you dummy!" I for one am glad it doesn't say that in the Bible. But too often we live as if it did—as if the name we've been given by our Creator had been crossed off our name tag and replaced with lies.

The last sentences of Jordan's story made my heart rejoice. "I no longer identify myself as an addict. Instead I say, 'Hello, my name is Jordan, and I'm a child of the one true King.'"

You have a choice today. A choice to decide which name tag you will wear. Let Jordan's story inspire you to lay down the lies and hold your head up high, knowing you are a child of the one true King!

Breaking Free

Now the Lord is the Spirit,
and where the Spirit of the Lord is, there is freedom.

2 Corinthians 3:17

Addictions can be killers. I'd hate to know the number of men and women who started out following God's will for their lives but were tempted by some substance or activity that eventually bound them in the chains of addiction. Those chains can bind us so tightly that they choke the life out of us.

Can you commit with me that Satan will not rob you of your destiny in God? Tell God you're His 100 percent—which leaves zero percent for any addictions or idols.

If you're already bound by an addiction, you can break free. Do whatever it takes. Start with prayer and total surrender to Christ. Then show you're serious by getting support as you walk out of your prison into freedom.

It's okay to pray, *God, I can't break free alone. I need Your help and the help of those who know how to counsel me and be there for me when I struggle with temptation.*

Friend, don't miss out on what God has for you. Every day can be your Day One of freedom in Christ. You get to make the decision. I'm praying for you.

Today Is DAY ONE

Clean Yourself Up

God demonstrates his own love for us in this:
While we were still sinners, Christ died for us.

ROMANS 5:8 NIV

My wife, Emily, and I have been married for 12 years. In the earliest stages of our dating relationship, I suffered an injury that landed me in the hospital for several days. My main concern while in that hospital bed wasn't my health. I was concerned about how I was going to look when Emily, my girlfriend at the time, came to visit me. Because let's face it—nobody looks good in a hospital gown! So before Emily's visit, regardless of how much pain I was in, I asked my mom to help me comb my hair and shave so I could make a good impression.

Looking back, I smile at the thought of how much I wanted to impress Emily. Knowing what I know now, it didn't really matter how I looked. I'm so thankful that Emily saw me at my worst and chose to love me anyway. And you know what—I'm thankful that the same is true with God. God loved us while we were still sinners.

You don't have to clean yourself up before coming to God. He's seen you at your worst and loves you anyway. He sent His Son to die for you.

Fresh Mercy

Blessed be the God and Father of our Lord Jesus Christ, the Father of mercies and God of all comfort.

2 Corinthians 1:3

I don't know how it is with you, but for me, I'm sure glad each day brings a fresh supply of God's mercy. I can start a day just fine—clean slate and all that—but before long I find myself in a tight spot. I might get frustrated at something or someone. That can trigger anger. Or sometimes even sadness.

Another incident comes along and triggers another reaction in me. I find myself thinking in a way that's definitely not from the Lord.

How about you? Ever blow up at someone when you didn't mean to? Or get down when things don't go your way?

If that's you now, or you find yourself that way later today, just stop in your tracks. Give God a little praise and receive His mercy and forgiveness. Then walk away from the situation until your emotions get stable again.

Thank You, Father, for fresh, fresh, fresh mercy!

Do Something

We are God's handiwork, created in Christ Jesus to do good works, which God prepared in advance for us to do.
EPHESIANS 2:10 NIV

Not long ago I sang at a benefit concert for an orphanage in Uganda started by a young woman named Andrea. She had traveled there as a college student, and during her semester abroad, God broke her heart about the plight of abused and neglected orphans. This college student from Colorado turned into an activist and decided to do something about those children. Her story inspired me to pen the song "Do Something."

> If not us then who
> If not me and you
> Right now
> It's time for us to do something

Today, Andrea lives in Iganga, Uganda. Her orphanage cares for more than 200 children daily and continues to inspire people to remember that each of us can do something.

Would you believe that God has planned opportunities for you to do great things today and reach out to this hurting world to show them His love? How do I know this? The Bible tells me so in Ephesians 2:10.

Ask God today if He would have you do something. Ask Him to keep your eyes open to a lost and hurting world, and you'll be amazed at all the opportunities you get today and tomorrow and every day to reach out and change the world.

Counting the Days

"What no eye has seen, nor ear heard,
nor the heart of man imagined,
what God has prepared for those who love him"—
these things God has revealed to us through the Spirit.

1 Corinthians 2:9-10

Remember how it was in school when summer break drew near? Or when Christmas was coming? Ten days till summer break! Seven days till Christmas! Three days till my birthday! Those holidays are great events, for sure. But have you ever thought about how many days you have until eternity?

There are 365 days in most years, and let's say I've got another 50 years on planet earth. That means in about 18,250 days (give or take a few thousand), I'll begin the biggest holiday of all.

You may have far fewer days left. Or maybe many more. But think how exciting it is to look forward to eternity with Christ and to count down the days until you're in His presence. That attitude makes every day exciting—knowing you're 24 hours closer to heaven. And just wait until you see what God has planned for you in eternity!

Don't Miss It

I have come that they may have life, and have it to the full.
John 10:10 NIV

A woman shared with me the story of her strained relationship with her dad. He had made one poor choice after another and was never the dad she needed him to be. As a result, they rarely ever spoke.

But at 80 years old, he found himself in the final days of his life. She wrote to me and said she went to be with him in the hospital because that's what daughters do.

While she was at his bedside, he looked up at her and he said, "I missed it, didn't I? I absolutely missed it."

That day a grown woman had the chance to hold her father's hand and pray with him as he asked Jesus into his heart for the first time.

After they prayed, she looked at her dad and said, "You're not missing it now—you've got it right now, and now is all we have."

Perhaps you've been tempted to think you've missed it. I pray that today's story does for you what it did for me. Make the choice not to wait another minute to turn your life over to the One who offers you life to the full. Ask God to help you live your life now in such a way that you reach the end with no regrets. Make sure you never have to say to someone, "I missed it, didn't I?"

Your life is waiting on you. Whatever you do, don't miss it.

Stop Beating Yourself Up!

Blessed are those whose...sins are covered.

ROMANS 4:7

Not long ago, I really blew it. I just lost it. I did or thought something that I regretted almost immediately. It should have come as no surprise to me though. See, I'm a human being. A man who is highly fallible.

The problem is that sometimes I make the mistake worse by beating myself up over what I did. Over my fallen humanity in action...once again. Here's what I should do:

1. Immediately acknowledge my sin to God.

2. Accept His forgiveness by faith.

3. Apologize to anyone who was in my path of destruction.

4. Move on, knowing God has forgiven me.

And here's the step I sometimes forget:

5. Stop beating myself up just because I failed.

God has forgiven me, so who am I not to forgive myself? Am I harder to please than God? Yeah, sometimes I think I am. God is quick to forgive me, but if I don't watch myself, I can still be berating myself for the same offense a week later.

Are you still beating yourself up from a long-forgiven failure or sin? Or even a recent one?

It's time to let yourself off the hook. You're forgiven by God. Now forgive yourself.

Your Family Tree

You intended to harm me, but God intended it all for good.
GENESIS 50:20 NLT

Rebecca told her heartbreaking story of the dysfunctional home she grew up in. Now as an adult, she was afraid to start a family of her own because she was convinced she was destined to become just another link in the chain of family dysfunction.

She described a poignant moment from her adult life. During a terrible argument in her parents' house, a family friend looked at her and said, "Well, I guess this is *your* legacy."

Rebecca responded, "Yeah, I guess so."

But she told me that in that moment, she felt that God was saying, *No, Rebecca, this is not your legacy. You have a new legacy because you are My child.* She told me that promise has made all the difference in her life.

Dysfunctional families are nothing new. Look at the story of Joseph in the Old Testament. He had such a dysfunctional family that his jealous brothers tried to kill him but wound up selling him off as a slave!

That family would have their own reality television show today! But we can learn from Joseph's perspective. Years later, he finally had an opportunity to face those who had hurt him the deepest. What did he say to them? "You intended to harm me, but God intended it all for good."

Perhaps you've come from a dysfunctional situation, just as Rebecca and Joseph did. If so, God's plan is to help you break those chains and establish a healthy new pattern. As you faithfully seek God, He will show you how He intends to turn your history into something good.

God's Day Planner

We walk by faith, not by sight.
2 CORINTHIANS 5:7

Have you ever wondered what God's day planner would look like? Especially the page that lists His plans for you? That's right—God has arranged a special day for you today. The truth is, every day is a specially designed day for those who trust in God. He can even make the things that seem to go wrong turn out just right.

That happens when we walk in faith. Everything on God's day planner is meant for our ultimate good. But sometimes we might not see the good until later.

Sometimes *much* later. The best way to understand the present events in our lives is to look back on them from the vantage point of the future. So regardless of what comes at you today, trust and praise God.

If I were to look in your day planner today, I hope I'd see the words "Live by faith today." That's really all you need to schedule a happy and successful day.

Today Is
DAY ONE

Forgiveness

Be kind and compassionate to one another, forgiving
each other, just as in Christ God forgave you.
EPHESIANS 4:32 NIV

It's the hardest thing to give away
The last thing on your mind today
And it always goes to those who don't deserve

I was inspired to write those words by Renee's story. She had to learn how to forgive a drunk driver named Eric who was responsible for taking the life of her beloved daughter. With the help of a forgiving God, she reached out to that young man, and his life is now forever changed. He came to a personal relationship with Christ because of the forgiveness he received from her. Today they travel around the country, speaking about the dangers of drunk driving and the power of forgiveness.

Not long ago, I stood inside the walls of a maximum-security prison and performed their song, "Forgiveness," for about 200 inmates. Renee was standing there with me, and so was Eric, who now visits that prison as a free man to show everyone what true freedom looks like.

I shed some tears that day as I saw a clear picture of how the prisoner in all of us can be set free by the power of one word—*forgiveness.*

Maybe you've got some forgiving to do today. Or maybe you need to ask someone for forgiveness. Maybe you just need a little help learning how to forgive yourself. I encourage you to spend some time today thinking and praying about that word—*forgiveness.* Ask God to show you the next steps He wants you to take in order to be free once and for all.

Today Is DAY ONE

Growing Each Day

Grow in the grace and knowledge of our Lord and Savior Jesus Christ.

2 Peter 3:18

When you were in school, third or fourth grade maybe, did you ever plant a few seeds in a small milk carton?

Your teacher probably had to remind you to water the seedling and to make sure it got some sun. After a few days, you saw your plant break through the dirt. It was just a little green thing at first, but almost day by day you could see it grow. If you watched it, you couldn't see it growing. It grew while you were doing other stuff—putting together a model airplane or eating supper or watching TV or sleeping.

If you were growing something like a carrot, you were tempted to pluck it up and see how big the carrot was. But that would have ruined everything.

Spiritual growth is like that. We need to grow in the Word and in prayer—that's like making sure the plant gets its water and sun—but we don't cause the growth. Only God can truly grow a Christian. And He does it slowly...Day One by Day One.

We get anxious and want to pull the carrot up, but that won't help. We just need to go about living for God, trusting our heavenly Father and spiritual growth will happen.

You will grow some today. You might not notice it, but that's okay. Every day, you grow a bit more into the Christian man or woman God wants you to be. Relax and enjoy the process.

The God of the Impossible

What is impossible with man is possible with God.

Luke 18:27

Aren't you thankful that God is in the business of making impossible things possible? He's done it throughout history, and He's still doing it today.

I was onstage at a recent concert when I noticed a woman holding up a big poster. Something prompted me to stop the show and walk out to her to read her poster. It read, "Cancer couldn't stop me from coming to see Matthew West. I'm a survivor!"

Tears filled my eyes as I looked into hers. There she was, raising her hands and worshipping the God of the impossible, right there in the middle of her seemingly impossible illness. The crowd joined me in praying for her that night. It was an amazing feeling to hear an entire crowd of people calling on the God of the impossible, trusting that He knows and loves this woman and will carry her through the rest of her treatment.

We will all come up against some seemingly impossible circumstances with seemingly impossible odds. But remember—we serve the God of the impossible!

Jesus made it clear: "What is impossible with man is possible with God."

Start your Day One with faith that you serve a God who specializes in making the impossible possible.

Today Is DAY ONE

Don't Put It Off

Do not let the sun go down while you are still angry.
EPHESIANS 4:26 NIV

I'm finally ready to admit I need a doctor. Like most guys, I can be pretty stubborn, especially when it comes to physical injury. This stubbornness can be traced back to haunting memories of high school football and the sound of my offensive line coach screaming, "You can play through pain if you're man enough, West!"

Do you think I'd hobble over to Coach and whimper, "Uh, yeah...um, I think I'm injured and better sit out these next couple of plays"?

No way! I chose to "suck it up," as my coach used to say, and get back on the field. I'm several years removed from the high school gridiron, but I still try to exercise as if I'm trying to be an all-state athlete. While attempting one too many pushups, I felt a shooting pain in my shoulder. Refusing to believe it could be anything serious, I decided to "suck it up," thinking a little rest was all I needed. Well, it's been weeks. And guess what? My shoulder hurts worse than it did in the beginning.

This stubbornness spills over into other aspects of my life as well, especially in my relationships. Instead of dealing with an issue, I tend to just let time pass, leaving words unsaid. I act as if time will heal the hurts I've caused or received. The Bible gives several encouragements to resolve conflict quickly. Yet pride or stubbornness gets in the way. Perhaps you have a relationship that has become complicated. Take it from the guy with the sore shoulder. Waiting won't heal what's broken. Don't let the sun go down today before taking some steps to resolve the conflicts in your life.

God's Purpose or Your Plans?

Many are the plans in the mind of a man,
but it is the purpose of the LORD that will stand.
PROVERBS 19:21

A young woman shared her story with me—how she'd worked so hard and planned everything out so she would be able to get her dream job. Well, just before beginning that dream job, she decided to take a mission trip. Here's what she wrote.

> During those ten days in Ghana, God broke my heart for ministry. I could no longer see myself working in the States. I knew what God's plan for my life was. At the end of this month, instead of pursuing my dream job, I have a new dream, and I will be heading to the mission field in Africa...I am scared of what this means for my life, but I'm so excited to be living in the center of God's will.

Choosing to forgo your own plans for God's purpose can be scary, uncertain, uncharted territory from our perspective. But the single most fulfilling place you'll ever find yourself is in the center of God's will.

Lay down your own plans today. Go to God and ask Him to show you your true purpose on this earth. It may be different from what you expected, but if you make the choice to pursue what He calls you to, you will find the life you were born to live.

Godly Ambition

What will it profit a man if he gains the
whole world and forfeits his soul?

MATTHEW 16:26

We all want to succeed in life, don't we? I know I do. I have ambitions. I want to be the best at what I do. I want people to be blessed by my life or my music. I love hearing about a life that was impacted after someone heard a song I wrote or attended one of my concerts.

But I have to be careful. Not all ambition is good. Worldly ambition can be a trap that squeezes the spiritual life out of us. I could want a million-dollar recording contract and a dozen Grammys—and though I'd be successful in the eyes of many, it wouldn't mean a thing if I lost God's anointing in the process. I'm sad to say I know people who have gained the world but lost their soul by compromising and by chasing success.

Here's the thing: God has given all of us talents. We all can do something. And we all can be tempted to use God's gifts as a means of getting applause from the world. That applause ringing in our ears can drown out the voice of God. It really can.

Today you have talents. What will you do with them? What is your ambition for life? Do you want the world's applause or God's approval? Rarely can you have both.

Don't squander your gifts on the kind of success that goes to the grave with you. Chase the success that reaps eternal rewards. You'll be happier not only in eternity, but in this life as well. Using God's gifts for ministry brings an inner joy and satisfaction the world can never provide.

Joy

You will fill me with joy in your presence.
PSALM 16:11 NIV

My all-time favorite movie is one that most people typically associate with the Christmas season. But not me! I watch *It's a Wonderful Life* all through the year. I've probably seen it more than 300 times!

In one of my favorite scenes, God has a conversation with an awkward, second-class angel named Clarence.

> CLARENCE: "You sent for me, sir?"
> GOD: "Yes, Clarence. A man down on earth needs your help."
> CLARENCE: "Splendid! Is he sick?"
> GOD: "No, worse. He's discouraged."

Billy Graham once said, "The Christian life is not a constant high. I have my moments of deep discouragement. I have to go to God in prayer with tears in my eyes and say, 'Help me.'"

Are you discouraged today? Maybe you're battling with depression. Maybe you can relate to the girl who wrote me recently from a college dorm room asking, "Why do I even exist?"

Psalm 16:11 says, "You will fill me with joy in your presence." Step into God's presence today. *Stay* in God's presence today. Pour out your heart to Him. He will bring you out of this darkness and show you how real His joy truly is.

Complete in Him

You are complete in Him,
who is the head of all principality and power.

COLOSSIANS 2:10 NKJV

I love this verse. I think the reason is that some days I don't feel very complete. In fact, I feel very incomplete. And yet this Scripture assures me that today—on this Day One—I am complete in Him.

Not complete in myself.

Not complete because of what I do today.

Not complete because of how I feel today.

Not complete because of what others think or say about me.

Not complete because of what I believe about myself.

No, my completeness is fully anchored in Him. And so is yours. You are complete in Christ on this Day One. And nothing can take that away from you.

Whatever comes your way on this Day One, I want you to know beyond the shadow of a doubt that God has created you, He has given you a special one-of-a-kind identity, and you are complete in Him.

A Day One Resolution

Not that I have already obtained all this, or have already arrived at my goal, but I press on to take hold of that for which Christ Jesus took hold of me. Brothers and sisters, I do not consider myself yet to have taken hold of it. But one thing I do: Forgetting what is behind and straining toward what is ahead, I press on toward the goal to win the prize for which God has called me heavenward in Christ Jesus.

PHILIPPIANS 3:12-14 NIV

Every December 31, the world anxiously awaits the beginning of a new year. We watch the ball drop and sing "Auld Lang Syne." And if you're like me, you jot down a New Year's resolution. So here I am, checking in on you to see how your New Year's resolution is going. If it's going anything like mine, it's already gone!

But come to think of it, a New Year's resolution isn't enough. I don't know about you, but I seem to be in need of a Day One resolution—a new one every day! Every single day I need to make a new commitment to put God first, trust Him with my life, and keep fighting the good fight.

Paul's words in Philippians 3:12-14 sound a little bit like a Day One resolution to me—especially the part about forgetting the past and pressing on toward the goal to win the prize.

Now *that's* a Day One resolution! Make it yours today.

Today's Eternal Value

Teach us to number our days
that we may get a heart of wisdom.
PSALM 90:12

When you're rich and you find a dollar bill, you don't think much about it. It's just a dollar. No biggie. But when you're dead broke and you find a dollar, you're excited. That dollar bill has more value when you're broke than when you're rich.

What about one happy, carefree day on earth? How much value do we place on that? If we're healthy, we may think, *It's just a day. No biggie.*

But if we're seriously sick—say, life-threateningly sick—we value one carefree day differently. In fact, if we begin the day deathly sick and by noon we're suddenly healthy, we're overjoyed. We hop out of bed laughing and crying for joy because we have another carefree day when we thought we were at death's door.

It's true—every day has true value. Even when we're sick, we're *here*. We can pray. We can thank God for each breath. We can even experience the love of God by trusting Him for our health tomorrow. What we can't afford to do is take a day—like today—for granted. Value today as if it were going to be the best day of your life.

No Conflicting Reports

God is light; in him there is no darkness at all. If we
claim to have fellowship with him and yet walk in
the darkness, we lie and do not live out the truth.

1 John 1:5-6 NIV

Some time ago, I attended the funeral of an older gentleman. As I sat with his friends, co-workers, and family members in the chapel, I listened as one by one they took turns saying a few words in tribute. The final person to speak was the gentleman's best friend. He stood up and said, "The most fitting tribute to our friend is that there are no conflicting reports today about what kind of man he was."

I've thought about those words often since that day at the funeral. *What if that could be said about me? What if I could live my life loving God and loving others with such authenticity that when I reach the end, there will be no conflicting reports?*

The Bible makes it clear that in Him there is no darkness. May our lives be held up to His light every day so there can be no conflicting reports about how we say we live and how we really live.

Ask God to show you any inconsistencies in your life and in your relationships. Make it your prayer that you get to the end of this day and the end of your life with no darkness and no conflicting reports.

Today's Fire

I baptize you with water for repentance, but
he who is coming after me is mightier than
I, whose sandals I am not worthy to carry. He
will baptize you with the Holy Spirit and fire.

MATTHEW 3:11

If you've ever camped out, you know the value of the campfire. You want to keep the embers burning through the night so when you wake up, the fire will quickly flame up again with a little fresh fuel. But sometimes you wake up and find the embers have burned out. All you have is yesterday's ashes, and you can't build a fire out of that.

Yesterday's ashes give evidence of yesterday's fire, but that's about all. For today's fire, you need fresh fuel, oxygen, and a spark. That's how God works with us. We get today's fire *today*. He won't give us ashes from yesterday for the fire we need today. Nor will He give us tomorrow's fire today.

We already have the fuel of His Word. We have the oxygen—prayer. We have the spark of His Holy Spirit living inside us. Those three in combination will build a fresh fire every Day One of your life.

Get alone with God. Get something from His Word—a verse, a promise, a nugget of revelation—and as you pray, let the Spirit of God ignite the fire for today. It will keep you warm all day long.

Peace

I am leaving you with a gift—peace of mind and heart.
And the peace I give is a gift the world cannot give.
JOHN 14:27 NLT

Recently I was in yet another airport, traveling to yet another concert. It was chaotic, as all airport terminals are. And that's when I noticed a sign promising 15 minutes of peace and serenity in the middle of this commotion—the chair massage.

I paid my money and sat down in that chair, hoping to find the peace I was looking for in the midst of this chaos. And guess what—I didn't find it!

That chair massage in the airport was about as relaxing as, well, a chair massage in an airport. But this is how it goes in our lives sometimes. We're traveling through everyday chaos, seeking a moment's peace wherever it's promised. And yet we remember the words of Jesus, and we remember that true peace can only come from one source. "I am leaving you with a gift—peace of mind and heart. And the peace I give is a gift the world cannot give."

You know where to find peace today. Go to Him, and you'll receive it.

Today Is DAY ONE

Take 26

This is my blood of the covenant,
which is poured out for many for the forgiveness of sins.
MATTHEW 26:28

Why do they put erasers on the end of pencils? You know the answer—because we make mistakes. We all need a good eraser on our pencil—and in our life.

When I go into a recording studio, I don't always get a song right on the first try. We do the first take, and I might blow it. So we go to take two. And three...four...five...six...

It's human to blow it. But God has a divine eraser. It's called forgiveness, and it operates in our lives because of the blood of Christ, which cleanses us from all sin. *All* sin.

When I was a boy, I'd use the pencil's eraser over and over and over. Finally, I had a pencil left but no eraser. I tore many pages of paper trying to get one more mistake erased when I had no more eraser. You too, right?

Well, good news. God's eraser never wears down. It erases completely but is never used up.

Can you begin this Day One with a clean slate by using God's eraser to take away your sins? Sure you can. You can be completely free from your sins by partaking of the blood of Christ. Confess those sins, receive God's forgiveness by faith, and then be empowered by the Holy Spirit, by whom you can walk in the Spirit and not give in to the pull of the flesh.

Start today clean—and be thankful for God's divine eraser that never runs out.

Population Me

Here I am. Send me.

Isaiah 6:8 NLT

I want to challenge you today to step outside of your own little world. Not long ago I posted the lyrics to my song "My Own Little World" on Facebook.

> What if there's a bigger picture?
> What if I'm missing out?
> What if there's a greater purpose
> I could be living right now
> Outside my own little world?

One woman's response made me laugh! She wrote, "I'm just trying to figure out what to make for dinner tonight! Can you challenge me tomorrow?"

Many of us start our days with a desire to have an eternal impact on our world, but then we get so caught up in the demands of daily life (like what to make for dinner) that we forget we're here for a greater purpose.

What if this was our prayer every day? "Here I am. Send me."

I believe God would show us how we can step outside our own little world and change the world by showing people the love of Christ. I find that when I put God first and really set out each day with a desire to make an impact in the world, I gain a greater understanding of what really matters, and my to-do list begins to change for the better.

So will yours.

Today Is DAY ONE

Little Things

There is a boy here who has five barley loaves and two fish, but what are they for so many?

JOHN 6:9

God is in the little things of life, not just the things we think of as big. We tend to overlook the little things, probably because we think God cares only about our big stuff—our career, our money, our relationships, our ministry. And He does care about those. But life is mostly made up of much smaller things. Some of those small things God wants to use. When Jesus wanted to feed the 5000 who had been following Him, He asked Philip where they could buy bread for the people. But according to John 6:6, "He said this to test him."

Philip replied that they didn't have enough money to buy bread for such a large crowd. But Andrew had an interesting reply. He joined the conversation by pointing out, "There is a boy here who has five barley loaves and two fish." But then he added, "But what are they for so many?"

In man's eyes, five loaves and two fish are not enough for 5000 men (plus women and children). It's too small an amount. But wait...aren't we talking about Jesus here? With Him, only a little is more than enough. With Jesus, little things can be multiplied.

Today, don't overlook the little things. Let God use them to build your faith.

Today Is DAY ONE

The Power of Prayer

The prayer of a righteous person is powerful and effective.
JAMES 5:16 NIV

A while back I received a story from a 13-year-old boy in California that reminded me of the power of prayer. He said, "Life used to be so hard because my dad wasn't a Christian but Mom was. They would fight and yell, and I would just stand in a corner crying."

Well, that little boy went to church one Sunday, and the pastor was taking prayer requests. The boy believed in the power of prayer, so he asked the church to pray for his dad to get saved. This is what he wrote happened next: "The pastor came to my family and talked to my dad. And man, what a talk! That very night my dad accepted Christ in his heart. My mom and my little brother cried for joy, and I just praised God with all my heart because God answered my prayer and brought my dad back to me."

Have you been praying for someone or something? Maybe you've been praying for a long time, and you wonder if God is even listening. James 5:16 says, "The prayer of a righteous person is powerful and effective." I encourage you to hit your knees today and tomorrow and the day after that, asking God to do the impossible—because we serve a God who can!

The Power of Adversity

If you faint in the day of adversity,
your strength is small.
PROVERBS 24:10

You may face unexpected adversity today. So what will you do with it? I know what I've done in the past. I've grumbled, kicked rocks down the road, maybe muttered a halfhearted prayer or two, and let my misery be known to all.

But I've learned two things about adversity. The first thing is that adversity eventually moves on. It doesn't stay forever. So I try to take this attitude: *Okay, so today is a day of adversity, and tomorrow might be too. Big deal. I'll live. I'll get through this. Adversity will move on.*

The second thing is that adversity has a positive power to it—when I accept it that way. Adversity becomes a teacher for me. It teaches me to be patient. To trust God. To forgive others. Lots of other stuff too.

Sometimes I think God allows adversity for that very reason. He wants us to learn something, and this present adversity is His lesson plan for the day. (Or week. Or month.)

Maybe there's a third thing about adversity: The sooner I learn to trust God in the midst of adversity, the sooner it moves on.

If you find yourself facing adversity today, don't grumble, don't get mad, and don't kick rocks down the road. Just trust God and wait adversity out. Don't let it win the contest by sidelining you. Stay in the game.

All Your Needs

My God will meet all your needs
according to the riches of his glory in Christ Jesus.
PHILIPPIANS 4:19 NIV

Are you in a season of having some very specific areas of need in your life? Well, if you're anything like me, regardless of how many times in the past God has provided for you at just the right time, it's easy to lose perspective and forget who your true provider is.

For some reason, I find it difficult to remember how faithful He always is and always has been. Philippians 4:19 serves up a much-needed reminder of God's faithfulness to meet our needs. Aren't you glad that the word *all* is in that Scripture? It doesn't say that God will meet the occasional need you have, not just some of your needs, and not even several of your needs. No, our God will meet *all* our needs according to His riches.

So bring your needs to God today, and do so with confidence. He already knows what your needs are. And truthfully, greater than any earthly need we might have today, our deepest need is Jesus. He longs to be with you, to talk with you, to shower His peace on you, and to remind you that today and every day He will supply all your needs.

Waiting in God's Line

Be still before the LORD and wait patiently for him.
PSALM 37:7

I don't like to wait. Do you? If I go to the bank or the post office and the line is long, I get impatient as I wait. Sometimes I think God must deliberately put me at the end of a long line just so I'll learn how to be patient. And maybe have time to pray. That's the thing about waiting—it forces us to be still and do something other than rush around the way we usually do.

Sometimes I'm waiting but not in a line. I'm waiting for God to open the next door for me or to speak to my heart about a problem I have. God seems to want His people to be experts at waiting. I think that's true because of all the opportunities to practice waiting He sends my way.

I'll probably have to wait in line somewhere today. Maybe you will too. While you're waiting, take some time off from your impatience. Pray for the person in front of you. Pray for the counter clerk. Pray for yourself. Pray for the open doors you've been waiting for. Pray for your country and its leaders.

We're all earning our merit badges in waiting—and no one gets to take cuts in God's line. We all have to wait our turn.

A Pure Heart

Create in me a pure heart, O God,
and renew a steadfast spirit within me.
PSALM 51:10 NIV

This is a fitting prayer you and I can pray at the beginning of every single day. "Create in me a pure heart, O God, and renew a steadfast spirit within me."

The Bible describes Satan as "the father of lies" (John 8:44), and the father of lies would love nothing more than to get you to believe that purity in your life is unattainable because you have made too many mistakes. This can be hard to fathom, but God can re-create a pure heart in us even after we've become impure. This is why Christ died on the cross. Isaiah 1:18 tells us, "Though your sins are like scarlet, I will make them as white as snow. Though they are red like crimson, I will make them as white as wool" (NLT).

Be encouraged today by this: There is no dirt God's grace can't wash away, no sin too great for God to forgive. He loves you. His truth can speak louder than those lies. So make this your prayer today: "Create in me a pure heart, O God, and renew a steadfast spirit within me." And know that this is a prayer God will always answer.

Today Is **DAY ONE**

Covered in Prayer

Pray without ceasing.

1 Thessalonians 5:17

I don't know how some people make it through the day without prayer. I don't mean just a "Bless my day, Lord" kind of prayer. I mean the kind of prayer that fully commits the day to God. Lots can happen today—and not all of it good. I travel many days of the year, and I have responsibilities that weigh on me. I also need to be creative by writing songs God gives me. I need physical energy and lots of discernment. I flat-out need the Lord every minute of every day. We all do.

Every Day One needs to be covered in prayer. *Covered* in prayer. Don't shortchange God by offering Him just a quick bullet prayer to heaven. Start the day by getting real with God. Praise Him, thank Him, tell Him you trust Him. Then make your needs for the day known. Yeah, He already knows them, but He wants to hear from you anyway. He wants you to *daily* depend on Him. If you love someone, you want to talk to them. That's what prayer is all about.

Today, don't walk out the door into an un-prayed-over day. Cover your day in prayer and offer it to the One who's got you covered every day.

Today Is DAY ONE

The Reason for the World

He will wipe every tear from their eyes.
There will be no more death or mourning or crying or pain.
REVELATION 21:4 NIV

Ryan was an awesome 18-year-old young man who loved God with all of his heart. He was tragically killed in a car accident on his way to college one morning. After his death, his parents discovered Ryan's Facebook page, and their hearts were filled with hope as they read his final post the night before his accident.

> I don't want to go through the motions
> I don't want to go one more day
> Without Your all-consuming passion inside of me

I was stunned when I heard this story because those are the lyrics to my song "The Motions." I immediately felt a strong connection to this special family as they mourned the loss of Ryan.

Ryan's mother wrote me on the first anniversary of losing their precious son. Her note said, "Our family is incomplete until we are together again someday in heaven."

We have a promise in Revelation 21:4 that God will wipe every tear from our eyes. There will be no more death or mourning or crying or pain.

When we reach the last day of our life on earth, it marks Day One of eternity, and oh, what a glorious day that will be!

Take Joy!

Rejoice in the Lord always;
again I will say, rejoice.

PHILIPPIANS 4:4

Day One is really tough when I have no joy. Maybe I woke up on the wrong side of the bed or I had a bad dream or I'm still carrying a burden from yesterday...for whatever reason, beginning Day One is harder when I have no joy.

So what's the answer? I know I can't manufacture joy on my own. I can ask God for joy, and sometimes that's helpful. Starting the day with a song in my heart can help—even if I have to force myself to find the right song. But when it comes right down to it, we just have to walk by faith for every step of our Christian life. We have to have joy by faith...even when we don't feel joyful.

We received our salvation by faith, and we receive our joy the same way. We trust. Regardless of what's around us, we trust. So I woke up on the wrong side of the bed. So I had a bad dream. So I'm still carrying yesterday's burden. Regardless of all this, the promise of joy is still mine. I can receive the joy of the Lord by faith. I get out of bed (right side or wrong side), I dismiss the troublesome dream, and I release yesterday's burden to the Lord...by faith. The result is that when I walk in joy by faith, joy soon overtakes me and turns Day One into a stepping-stone to my destiny.

Today Is DAY ONE

Seek with All Your Heart

*You will seek me and find me when you
seek me with all your heart.*

JEREMIAH 29:13 NIV

One of my favorite Bible verses is Jeremiah 29:11, "'For I know the plans I have for you,' declares the LORD, 'plans to prosper you and not to harm you, plans to give you hope and a future'" (NIV). What an incredible promise! But recently I read past that well-worn verse during my quiet time. Truthfully, I sometimes read the Bible as if I'm listening to a "greatest hits" record of my favorite singer. I hit the highlights, focusing on those banner verses we hear so much in church or we committed to memory in vacation Bible school. But every word of Scripture is God-breathed. We can often gain greater insight and meaning when we dig a little deeper and read a little farther. For example, if we continue past Jeremiah 29:11, we read, "Then you will call on me and come and pray to me, and I will listen to you. You will seek me and find me when you seek me with all your heart."

Isn't it wonderful knowing that God has a plan for your life and that it's a plan to prosper you and not to harm you? Absolutely! But naturally, the next question is, how do I go about finding out what that plan is?

Thankfully, these verses offer that answer. God knows the plans He has for you, and He is calling you not to seek out that plan, but to seek Him with all your heart. The promise is written, and the promise is clear. *You will find Him when you seek Him with all your heart.* And as you do that, God will continue to reveal to you His plan for your life.

Today Is
DAY ONE

Thank God for My Weakness

For the sake of Christ, then, I am content with weaknesses, insults, hardships, persecutions, and calamities. For when I am weak, then I am strong.

2 CORINTHIANS 12:10

Sometimes I'm tempted to wish I had no weaknesses. Just think of how great it would be to be strong in every area of your life...or would it?

To be honest, my weaknesses drive me to the Lord every single day. Without my weaknesses, I would be tempted to walk through life in my own strength. I would have no need for the Lord at all. I would be self-sufficient.

When I think about it, that's a scary thought—to live like I have no need of the Lord because I have the strength in myself to meet every need that comes up.

I suppose some people actually feel that way, and there are many times when I am one of them. I know how weak I am. And in case I ever forget, God sends situations my way that remind me how much I need Him on every single Day One.

Thank You, God, for my every weakness. For in them, I discover Your strength working through me.

Tickets to the Gun Show

They that wait upon the LORD shall renew their strength;
they shall mount up with wings as eagles;
they shall run, and not be weary;
and they shall walk, and not faint.

ISAIAH 40:31 KJV

One of the most intimidating places for me to visit is the gym. Know what I mean? I walk in and see all these guys with huge muscles, perfectly sculpted guns, and protein shakes in hand. Meanwhile, I walk in with my baggy sweatshirt and chicken legs.

Yes, going to the gym and staying in shape can be intimidating and quite a struggle. Wouldn't it be awesome if all we had to do was just show up at the gym and get a ripped body without lifting a single weight or setting foot on the treadmill?

We all know that, unfortunately, it doesn't work like that. We've got to pick up those weights; we've got to get on that treadmill. Showing up is only half the battle when it comes to conquering physical fitness. But while simply waiting might not work at the gym, waiting is a key to *spiritual* fitness. Isaiah 40:31 says, "They that wait upon the LORD shall renew their strength; they shall mount up with wings as eagles; they shall run, and not be weary; they shall walk, and not faint."

Join me in making a renewed commitment to grow in strength spiritually. Wait on the Lord, and He will renew your strength.

Learning to Love

Love one another earnestly from a pure heart.
1 Peter 1:22

The true mark of a Christian is love. Not just the kind of shallow love we think of when we say, "Don't ya love that new TV show?" or "I love this hot fudge sundae!" I mean the deeper kind of agape love that God calls every one of us to exhibit. Even when it's hard. God says in His Word that anyone can love those who love them back. It takes a special kind of love to be able to love those who disagree with us or are our bitter enemies.

That kind of love for others doesn't come naturally to most of us. It sure doesn't to me. But God is able to love others through me with that kind of love...if I let Him. I've noticed He even sends certain people my way who are naturally hard to love. That's why it takes His supernatural love working through me to make a difference in my life and in theirs.

Okay, time to fess up. You know a person (or two or three...) who is hard for you to love, right? Then be honest with God and admit you can't love this person the way you should. Then ask Him to love that person through you. Next, begin to pray for that person whenever you think about them. Pray for them to be blessed. Pray for some kind of reconciliation with them.

I know from experience how much better every Day One can be when we operate out of love for others. God's love—not our own.

Give it a try.

Today Is DAY ONE

Are You a Story Keeper or a Storyteller?

And they overcame him by the blood of the Lamb,
and by the word of their testimony.

REVELATION 12:11 KJV

Your life is a powerful story that God is writing. But a story has power only when it's told. So the question is, will you be a story *keeper* or a story*teller*? Revelation 12:11 tells us the accuser (Satan) was overcome "by the blood of the Lamb, and by the word of their testimony."

Notice two things that defeat the accuser. The "blood of the Lamb" and "the word of their testimony." Your testimony—your story—is powerful enough to defeat Satan and his lies. But if you choose to keep your story to yourself and never tell it, your story will be robbed of its power, and that is exactly what the accuser wants to happen.

He pursues a world full of hurting people, trying to make them believe that God couldn't possibly love them—that God couldn't possibly change their life.

Well, if you know that's a lie, and if God has changed your life, it's not enough just to live your story. Go out and *tell* your story so that this lost and broken and hurting world can see the proof that God's love never ends.

Maybe you've never told your story before. Well, there's no better time to start than right now! This is Day One.

Thank God for Today

It is God who works in you,
both to will and to work for his good pleasure.

PHILIPPIANS 2:13

If we believe God has a plan for us, we also have to believe that each and every new day brings circumstances that are moving us on in God's plan. Maybe when you're young, you can't look back very far and see how God has worked in your life. But with each passing year, you can see how far you've come from where you used to be. You can see that literally *every day* matters in God's plan for you. Sure, some days seem to roll by just like the previous day and the day before that, but that's from your very limited human point of view. God usually chooses to work incrementally with us. We can't normally see from one day to the next how we've changed.

Here's the thing: Trust God for this particular Day One. Thank Him for it. Whether you realize it or not, God is at work in you...today. Even if you don't see it. And today might become one of those days you look back on years from now and remember a certain way that God spoke to you, provided for you, or helped you grow in a special way.

Thank You

Give thanks in all circumstances;
for this is God's will for you in Christ Jesus.

1 THESSALONIANS 5:18 NIV

Calling all complainers! You know who you are, because I know who I am. I can complain with the best of them. Nine out of ten things could be going perfectly well in my life, and guess what I'm going to focus on—that one thing that's not quite right.

When my youngest daughter, Delaney, was first learning to talk, she seemed to pick up one phrase in answer to everything—"Thank you." But when she tried to say it, her *Th*'s and *Y*'s sounded more like *D*'s, so it was "dank do." This seemed to be her response to any question.

"Delaney, did you have a nice nap?" "Dank do."

"Delaney, don't climb into the dishwasher." "Dank do."

"Delaney, that is one stinky diaper!" "Dank do."

Sounds crazy, I know, but maybe Delaney was on the right track in terms of how we should live our lives every day—with a spirit of thankfulness. First Thessalonians 5:18 (NIV) says, "Give thanks in all circumstances; for this is God's will for you in Christ Jesus."

Let's be like Delaney—let's make "thank you" two of our most frequently spoken words. Let's give thanks to God in any circumstance.

What If?

Do not fear, only believe.

MARK 5:36

Have you noticed how Satan attacks us through fear? The result is that fear can undermine our Day One. Fear destroys our confidence in God's work. Sometimes fear works this way in my life: *What if I lose the ability to write songs? What if I get a serious illness? What if the economy collapses? What if God is mad at me?* And so on. Satan knows the particular fears to pitch our way in hopes of sidetracking us. And all of them begin with those two words, *What if...?*

When Satan whispers those words, it's like he's planting seeds in our minds. We need to pluck them up immediately, or they'll grow into full-blown obsessive fears that undermine our faith and paralyze us.

Here's the best remedy. Whenever you hear those two words, turn them around into statements of faith. *What if God blesses my plans to serve Him? What if I prosper in my job and am promoted? What if God brings happiness and fulfillment to my entire family?* And my favorite: *What if my best songs have yet to be written? What if God uses them to change thousands of lives?*

Let this be Day One of no longer fearing Satan's whispers, but of believing God for a great future.

Today Is
DAY
ONE

The Works of God on Display

This happened so that the works of God
might be displayed in him.

JOHN 9:3 NIV

Tim was born with cerebral palsy. He approached me as I walked off the stage after a concert in Georgia, and we struck up a conversation. We talked about our love for baseball and gave each other a hard time when we found out we were fans of rival teams. Then he said, "I want to tell you my favorite Bible verses. In John 9:1-3 the disciples passed by a blind man and asked Jesus why he was born blind. I love Jesus's answer to them! He said that the man was born blind so the works of God might be displayed through him." Tim had a huge grin on his face as if to say, "I can relate to that blind man."

Tim's hands are crippled. I watched him use one hand to push the other out of the way for our picture, jokingly shouting to his hand, "Down, boy!" Tim is confined to his wheelchair, and he's had more surgeries than he can count. But he's not asking why. Instead, he's asking *how*. "How is God going to display His works through me today?"

What a perspective! What a challenge to look at life the way Tim does. I told Tim that was exactly what I sensed when I first saw him. I saw the power of God and the joy of the Lord.

I challenge you to ask God to give you Tim's perspective today. Instead of being like the disciples and asking why, ask God *how*.

Lord, how are You going to display Your work through me today?

Today Is

DAY ONE

Speaking Up

When they saw the boldness of Peter and John, and perceived that they were uneducated, common men, they were astonished. And they recognized that they had been with Jesus.

ACTS 4:13

The book of Acts reveals that one sign of being filled with the Spirit of God is boldness. Some of us wonder how that can be true of us. It's just not our nature to be bold, to speak up, or to be evangelists. Sometimes it scares us. We don't know what to say or how to say it.

And yet God has something that only you can say to your friends, relatives, neighbors, folks at church, and so on. Through the Holy Spirit, God will set up divine encounters, give us the right words to say, and empower us with the right amount of boldness to speak up in a geniune and impactful way.

Each Day One will likely offer a chance for you to speak a word of encouragement, comfort, or testimony to someone who needs to hear it. Someone God has placed in your path at that minute, hour, and day.

Don't be afraid. Let God use you. Speak up and trust that God will give you the words.

The Key Finder

*Forget the former things;
do not dwell on the past.
See, I am doing a new thing!*

Isaiah 43:18-19 NIV

One year a friend who knows me all too well gave me an almost perfect Christmas gift. It was one of those "as seen on TV" key finders. You know the kind—designed for people who are always forgetting where they left their keys so they'll never lose them again.

It was an *almost* perfect gift because nothing in the manual explained to people like me what to do when you lose the keys *and* the key finder. This is the story of my life! But when it comes to my past—my sins, the mistakes I've made—I never forget those. I remember them all too well.

And the enemy is right there to kick me while I'm down, reminding me of how many mistakes I've made. But then I remember Isaiah 43:18-19—"Forget the former things, do not dwell on the past. See, I am doing a new thing!" (NIV).

That's right—God is doing a new thing in your heart and in my heart. We don't need to dwell on the past anymore. God is doing a new thing, and today is Day One.

Now, if you'll excuse me, I've got some keys to find!

Cutting Loose Your Past

And he said to her, "Your sins are forgiven."
LUKE 7:48

Every single person on the planet has one thing in common—a past. My past may not look like yours. Yours may not look like your neighbor's or your pastor's or even your own sibling's. Some people have a fairly tame past with seemingly few regrets. Others have a seriously troubled past—perhaps because of sins other people committed against them, or maybe because of their own poor choices, or possibly because of circumstances beyond their control.

The great thing about Day One is that none of that really matters. Tame pasts are *past*. Seriously troubled pasts are *past*. Many Christians go on day after day, year after year trying to escape a troubled past—often to no avail.

That is never God's plan. As a loving Father, God has made provision for every past imaginable. He is the God of forgiveness of sins, the God of restoration, the God of healing, the God of new beginnings. We never need to carry our past into our present or into our future.

Make the choice to cut loose of your past. Be free. That's what Day One is all about. Make the most of it.

A Lamp to Guide My Feet

Your word is a lamp to guide my feet
and a light for my path.

PSALM 119:105 NLT

Last year I made a commitment to read through the entire Bible in a year. I downloaded a nifty app and signed up for a yearlong reading program. I started out with great intention and faithfulness. And then I missed a day. And then I missed another day. And then the app sent me an e-mail that I'd fallen behind. *Hint, hint.*

It's easy to get discouraged when we stray from our routine or we allow our to-do list to knock off the most important part of our day—spending time in Scripture, spending time with the Lord. Thankfully, that app gave me a helpful option: "Catch me up." With one click, I was able to pick up where I left off without being constantly reminded of my missed days.

Count today as Day One. Let God's Word be a lamp to guide your feet and a light for your path.

We simply can't experience everything God has for us each day without spending time with Him and spending time in His Word.

Don't Try Harder

I am the vine; you are the branches. Whoever abides in me and I in him, he it is that bears much fruit, for apart from me you can do nothing.

JOHN 15:5

If you want to make God laugh, just tell Him, "I'll try harder, Lord." That can refer to promises about...

Giving up an addiction.

Not losing our temper.

Eating more healthy.

Getting into the Word.

Praying more.

_____ . (Add your promise here.)

I think God laughs at our attempts to try harder because He's seen it all before. And He's seen it from *us*. We've tried harder in the past and failed. What makes us think we'll be successful this time?

God doesn't want us to try harder. He wants us to overcome by *resting* more deeply. That's right. Rest deeply. Give yourself over to resting in Christ. Empty yourself of your own limited strength and draw deeply from Him.

Let this be Day One of your rest in God. Remember that you are free to live apart from the pressure of trying harder to please God. What pleases Him is when His children rest and abide in Him.

Transformed

Do not conform to the pattern of this world,
but be transformed by the renewing of your mind.
ROMANS 12:2 NIV

I received a story from a young man named Rusty. He wrote about growing up in church but making some poor decisions in his teenage years. He eventually turned to a life of crime and wound up in jail.

He told me that the day he was locked behind bars marked a turning point in his life. He realized he didn't want to be known simply by a cell number, and that's when God put a different number on his heart. That number was 180.

Rusty knew it was time to make a change in his life. He got out of jail, and with a renewed commitment to Christ, he began changing other people's lives as well. He now runs a nonprofit ministry called the 180 Zone. He's reaching out to people who are in the same crisis situation he faced, and he's showing them what true life change looks like.

Rusty's life has been transformed by a renewing of his mind—by a 180-degree turnaround.

Is it time for a turning point in your life?

Follow Rusty's lead, and God will change your life. Then, step into each Day One knowing that a transformed life can be used by God to transform other people's lives too.

Praise Breaks

I will bless the LORD at all times;
his praise shall continually be in my mouth.

PSALM 34:1

Every day is a "praise God" day. Sure, we go about our work or school or family stuff, and sometimes God isn't at the center of our attention. All those things are important, but even when we're not conscious of them, we need to know God is directing our life...yes, even in the small things. The mundane.

When a day is full of stuff that might cause me to forget the Lord, I find it necessary to enjoy a few praise breaks throughout my day. I try to either stop what I'm doing and just give God a little praise before continuing, or if I can't stop what I'm doing, I still praise God as I stay busy. It doesn't take much to just turn our attention to Him and say, "Lord, You're great. I love You and I praise You. Thank You for loving me today and every day. May Your name be praised."

Try it. Ask God to remind you a few times today to turn your mind toward Him in thanksgiving and praise.

Make this Day One a "praise God" day.

Winning Streaks

The steadfast love of the LORD never ceases;
his mercies never come to an end;
they are new every morning;
great is your faithfulness.

LAMENTATIONS 3:22-23

Recently the University of Connecticut women's basketball team held a streak of 90 victories—the longest in college basketball (men or women). Eventually that streak came to an end. Now, can you imagine what would have happened if after the losing game, the coach and the team sat in the locker room and decided to forfeit the rest of their season because their streak was over? That would be crazy, right?

But isn't that how we tend to go about our lives and our spiritual journeys? I get so caught up in trying to keep a winning streak as a Christian. If I haven't made many mistakes, I feel pretty good about myself. But the moment I mess up, fall short, lose my temper, forget to read my Bible, or do anything else to ruin my winning streak, I get discouraged, and I'm tempted to quit. That's why I'm thankful for verses like Lamentations 3:22-23, which remind me that God's mercies never come to an end.

God knows that we are incapable of perfection. He's not calling you to try to keep up a spiritual winning streak. His mercies are new this morning. And tomorrow morning they'll be new again. And the morning after that.

As you step into this Day One, remember God's fresh offering of new mercy.

The Lure of the World

Do not love the world or the things in the world.
If anyone loves the world, the love
of the Father is not in him.

1 JOHN 2:15

We start each Day One with promise and hope. We love the Lord and expect great things from Him—and rightly so. And then something we don't expect happens and starts to smother our hopes and expectations. Almost without warning, we're attracted to something of this world that is contrary to our faith. It assaults our attempts to live out a fresh Day One, and it threatens to consume tomorrow as well.

What are these things of the world that lure us away from Christ? They're probably different for different people. For some, certain kinds of entertainment can choke our spiritual life. For others, it's an obsessive interest in some activity that under normal circumstances is purely innocent. Sports, maybe. Or a worldly ambition on the job that involves compromise. For some Christians it can even be another person. You "fall in love" with a non-Christian who has no interest in your faith but who has deep roots in this present world. He or she says nice things to you and about you. So almost without realizing it, you enter into a compromising relationship that can only mean trouble.

Make no mistake about it, the lure of the world is strong. I get that. You need deep roots in Christ to withstand Satan's tantalizing bait. Is the love of the Father in you? If so, then the power of God is also in you. His power will give you the strength to recognise the lures of the world for what they are and will keep your heart close to Him.

A Work in Progress

Being confident of this very thing, that He who has begun a good work in you will complete it until the day of Jesus Christ.

PHILIPPIANS 1:6 NKJV

As a songwriter, I can never stop tweaking or working on the songs I've written. I'm always trying to make each lyric more unique, or digging for a better melody that will carry those lyrics to peoples' ears in the most enjoyable way.

Yes, I confess. I'm a perfectionist. I find it impossible to settle with my first draft. Instead, I'm constantly refining it all the way up until the last day when my producer says, "ENOUGH ALREADY! We've got to send this out to the radio station."

Well, that's how it is in our lives—God never stops working in us. He's a perfectionist too. He's constantly molding us and shaping us so we look more like Him and sing a beautiful song of salvation.

Don't get discouraged today if you're not where you think you should be. Philippians 1:6 reminds us that the One who began a good work in us "will complete it until the day of Jesus Christ" (NKJV). Notice, this Scripture is clear that God began the good work in you, but He's not finished with you yet. So keep going, keep seeking Him, and He'll show you who He wants you to be. He'll be faithful to complete the good work He has begun, and He will lead you to become the person He created you to be all along.

Today Is DAY ONE

Temptation

No temptation has overtaken you that is not common to man. God is faithful, and he will not let you be tempted beyond your ability, but with the temptation he will also provide the way of escape, that you may be able to endure it.

1 Corinthians 10:13

Isn't it amazing how Satan knows the exact points of temptation for every person he wants to capture for himself? For instance, there are some things that never tempt me. But I do have temptations, and Satan has designed those temptations just for me. They might never tempt you. They may be totally different from the things that tempt you. Temptations aren't contagious.

Temptations have one purpose—to draw us away from Christ, to trip us up. But God has a goal in our temptations too. Our temptations provide God with opportunities to reveal His overcoming power as we resist those temptations by trusting fully in Him.

I have a hunch on this Day One you're going to face some temptations. Some of which may be very severe. But no matter how strong your temptations, they are no match for the power of God working through a believing Christian.

Maybe yesterday you gave in to a temptation. Okay, it happened. Guess what? You're forgiven in Christ. Today is Day One for you. It's not yesterday. Yesterday is history. God's mercy is new for you today. You have a fresh opportunity to show God's power over your temptations.

The Rat Race

I pondered the direction of my life,
and I turned to follow your laws.

PSALM 119:59 NLT

Too often, we get so caught up in the chaos of doing life that we forget to stop and take inventory of what it is that we're doing and where the road we're on is taking us.

The demands of the day have a tendency to dictate our actions. If we don't pay attention, we may find ourselves no longer seeking God's will, but rather checking off the to-do list that our families, jobs, finances, or relationships have created for us.

Some might call it the rat race, the grind, or the hamster wheel. I'm not sure why so many of the analogies for this kind of living deal with rodents, but that alone motivates me to break free from that sort of busy, routine living!

God wants to reveal His plan for your life. And His plan might mean doing some things a little differently today than you may have planned. This is one of the most difficult tasks for a Christian—to check your motives at the door every single day and ask your Creator, *Is this the direction You want me to go?*

Don't just race blindly through your day. I challenge you to take a few moments to "ponder the direction" of your life. Ask God either to confirm that you are on the right path or to show you that this is Day One of His new direction for you.

If You Could Not Fail

The righteous falls seven times and rises again.
PROVERBS 24:16

What would you attempt if you knew you could not fail? Write a book? Go on the mission field? Start a band? Run for political office?

Fear of failure has stopped many Christians from attempting great things for God. Don't let that be the story of your life. Your Day One has some super possibilities to launch you into God's destiny. Don't miss out. Don't worry about failure. The truth is, you may stumble a bit. You may fail in man's eyes, but from God's point of view, failure happens only when we give up pursuing His will and quit moving forward.

I don't know what your calling is. Mine is music. I've had some failures along the way, but I'm still here. Still writing my songs, still ministering when I can, and still fulfilling God's destiny for me. I haven't given up...and I don't plan to.

What about you? Will you commit on this Day One to keep working toward your goal, knowing that in God's eyes you cannot fail?

Today Is DAY ONE

86,400 Seconds

Teach us to realize the brevity of life,
so that we may grow in wisdom.
PSALM 90:12 NLT

How many seconds are in 24 hours? 86,400. How do I know that? I googled it. But I don't need the Internet to teach me that each second is a gift, and not a single one is promised. So how will you spend your seconds today? If you're anything like me, you know how easy it is to get lulled into letting the seconds tick by before realizing that you've spent them on things that don't matter. Television, iPhone games, Facebook, and a multitude of other things vie for our attention and often pull us away from what's most important. The enemy would love nothing more than to get you to waste your seconds today on things that don't matter for eternity.

Don't let today's seconds run out before taking care of first things first. Commit some of your seconds every day to rest in God's presence. Time spent with God is never time wasted—it's time *invested*, and invested wisely.

Making the most of your 86,400 seconds starts with asking God to help you do just that. When you get off track, whisper a prayer and ask God to set your sights and focus on things that matter.

Setbacks

Who shall separate us from the love of Christ? Shall tribulation, or distress, or persecution, or famine, or nakedness, or danger, or sword?

ROMANS 8:35

Expect success on this Day One. Really. God wants you to succeed in following Him. But you know what? We're imperfect people. We mess up. Sometimes things happen beyond our control. The result is setbacks.

Setbacks can discourage us if we don't remember that God sees every setback. He knew it was coming, He was there when it happened, and He can handle the results. In fact, by faith, we can see God move on our behalf even as we suffer setbacks. It's a familiar saying but nonetheless true—our setbacks can become stumbling blocks or stepping-stones. Don't be discouraged if you have a setback today. Look up and give thanks to the God who sees. He can fix it. He can make it a useful stepping-stone. Get ready to set foot on it and move ahead. How you respond to your setbacks today will be the true deciding factor between success and failure.

Today Is DAY ONE

The Lord Has Been Good

Let my soul be at rest again,
for the LORD has been good to me.

PSALM 116:7 NLT

Every Thanksgiving, families all over the country gather around a dinner table for a celebratory meal. And like many families, mine has engaged in a tradition of each family member saying what he or she is thankful for. During this special time, there are plenty of smiles, laughs, and even cheers when our children tell us what they're thankful for. In those moments, our thoughts are focused not on what we lack, but on all that God has provided.

Oh, if only we could carry that feeling of rest and gratitude away from the Thanksgiving table and into our everyday lives. Yet too often our brief moments of rest are far outnumbered by hours and days, weeks and lives spent in a state of unrest. I love how this scripture from Psalms reminds us that rest and gratitude are connected. One creates the other. When I take time to focus on all the ways "the LORD has been good to me," my thankfulness takes up the space once occupied by worry, stress, discontentment, complaining, and negativity.

Don't wait for that one day a year that has the word *thanks* in its title. Take a few moments today and every day to actually count your blessings—to think about and even write down the ways God has been good to you. When you do this, your soul will find much-needed rest. And that rest will be one more thing to give thanks for.

Treasure Hunt

> The kingdom of heaven is like treasure hidden in a field,
> which a man found and covered up. Then in his joy
> he goes and sells all that he has and buys that field.
>
> MATTHEW 13:44

Did you love treasure hunts when you were a kid? I did. I still do. But the greatest hunt of all is to be found in the pages of the Word. The Bible is, in fact, like a grand treasure map, pointing us on every page to the greatest treasure of all—Jesus.

We can find Jesus, our treasure, every day. First, of course, we find Him in the Word. But then as we go about our day, we will find Him time and again if we really look for Him.

Make this Day One a treasure hunt. Look for Jesus at work in your daily life. Watch for His invisible hand as it weaves His will for you into today's events.

A treasure hunt fills the mind and heart with great anticipation of what one might find. A day in the life of a Christ follower can be filled with that same exciting anticipation for the treasures God will reveal to you.

Hello, My Name Is Defeat

Therefore, if anyone is in Christ, he is a new creation.
The old has passed away; behold, the new has come.

2 Corinthians 5:17

Recently, my father and I invited a group of young men who were going through the Teen Challenge drug recovery program to be our guests at a show. My dad is a pastor, and together we've started a ministry to people who need encouragement but are unable to attend concerts.

This particular night, a group of about 30 young men arrived in their matching polo shirts, excited to have a night out at the concert. I got to spend a few moments talking and praying with them before walking onstage.

But my dad had one painful interaction with a young man who was about 18 years old. My dad jokingly said, "You better watch out—there are lots of girls at these concerts, and you're looking really sharp in your polo shirt. They're gonna be asking for your phone number!"

The young man smirked but then hung his head. "Nah, none of these girls want anything to do with an addict like me." My dad looked that young man in the eyes and reminded him that God's plan for his life is far from over and that defeat does not define his identity.

If you are in Christ, then Christ lives in you! His promise to you is that the old is gone and the new has come. The devil wants you to hang your head in defeat as he reminds you over and over of your sins, your past, your regrets. Leave the old behind you, where it belongs. And then, every day and by God's grace, take up your God-given identity as a new creation.

Walking on Water

[Jesus] said, "Come." So Peter got out of the boat
and walked on the water and came to Jesus.

MATTHEW 14:29

Every Day One brings us new opportunities to walk on water—to move forward into the unknown with our eyes on Jesus. If we glance away, our faith will falter, and we will sink. But if we keep our eyes and our lives focused on Jesus, we'll accomplish more than we ever imagined.

Peter started well, but looking at the rough waters caused him to start sinking.

We all have our own rough waters to walk on. Maybe it's our financial situation, our challenging marriage, our job loss, our tragedies, or some other rough water that pulls our eyes away from Jesus. But Peter shows us that if we'll be brave enough to get out of the boat and walk toward Jesus—focusing on Him and not the storm around us—we'll succeed.

Watch for it today. Your opportunity to walk on water will surely come. When it does, get out of the boat, keep your eyes fixed on Jesus, and keep walking.

Today Is DAY ONE

No More Tryin'

The LORD doesn't see things the way you see them.
People judge by outward appearance,
but the LORD looks at the heart.

1 SAMUEL 16:7 NLT

When our tour bus parked in front of a little coffee shop in Omaha, it looked like a 747 parked in a backyard. I stepped off the bus and walked inside to meet a high school senior named Michaela. She is one of more than 40,000 people who have told me their story, and her story inspired a song on my *Live Forever* album.

Moved by a song I sang called "Hello, My Name Is," she wrote, "Hello, my name is Ugly." She wrote about her struggle with self-image due to the mean looks and harsh words from other girls who constantly made her feel as if she didn't measure up to their standards of beauty. Her self-esteem plummeted. But a friend invited her to a church youth retreat, and she agreed to attend. During the retreat, God began to work in her life in a powerful way. She discovered what the Bible says about her true beauty, and she left that retreat with a renewed faith and a resolve to believe the promises in Scripture instead of the lies of her so-called friends.

As we talked for the first time in that crowded coffee shop, Michaela shared with me her new desire to help other girls who battle a skewed self-image. She has combined her love of photography with her passion to share what she's learned by giving free photo shoots to other high school girls so they too can discover their true beauty as God's creations.

Have you seen yourself as beautiful in God's eyes? Because you are.

No Condemnation

There is therefore now no condemnation
for those who are in Christ Jesus.

ROMANS 8:1

Nothing can mess up Day One more than a cloud of guilt or condemnation. Thank God, He gives us the perfect remedy in Jesus Christ, our Redeemer from sin and its aftermath of guilt and condemnation.

Unfortunately, even after some people come to know Christ, they continue to carry a sense of condemnation. That weight will ruin anyone's Day One.

Let's get rid of that right now, okay? Here's the thing: Christ bore all your sins on the cross. All of them. No wonder the word *gospel* means "good news." In fact, it's terrific news—you no longer bear the weight of any of your sins. They are all gone! Forever dealt with at Calvary.

So why do we sometimes still feel guilty? Because we accept the enemy's lie that we are still guilty of our sins regardless of what Christ did on the cross. Can you imagine how such a thought cheapens what Christ did for us? Make no mistake about it—if you're not enjoying the full benefits of Christ's sacrifice for your sins, you're allowing Satan to have a foothold in your life, and he will attack you with his lies. But if you really "get" the fullness of forgiveness that Christ offers, you can easily dismiss Satan and his lies and rest in the joys of a fully forgiven life.

On this Day One, let all that guilt and condemnation go. Thank Christ for taking it away, and enjoy feeling completely free.

The Thief on the Cross

And he said, "Jesus, remember me when you come into your kingdom." And [Jesus] said to him, "Truly, I say to you, today you will be with me in Paradise."

Luke 23:42-43

Time and time again in Scripture, we see God offering His grace to the outcasts, the lost causes, and the down-and-out. And there is no more powerful display of grace than the dialogue between Jesus as He was being crucified on a cross and the thief on the cross beside him.

"Jesus, remember me when you come into your kingdom," the man cried.

These were the desperate words of a guilty criminal in the final seconds of his broken life. There was no use in defending himself. He was guilty and sentenced to die. There was no use in arrogance. The thief on the third cross took that approach, using his final angry breaths to hurl insults at Jesus.

There wasn't time for the thief to revisit his sins and ask for forgiveness. Besides, Jesus already knew. The man must have seen something in Jesus's eyes that day—a compassion that made his heart cry out with such a bold request.

This criminal's final day became his Day One as he soaked in Jesus's answer to his request. "Truly, I say to you, today you will be with me in Paradise."

Have you ever wondered, *Is it too late for me?* Take comfort today in knowing that paradise is promised to anyone who turns to Jesus at *any* time. You are never too old or too far gone to be forgiven. He remembered the thief on the cross, and He will remember you.

No Hypocrisy

Put away all malice and all deceit and
hypocrisy and envy and all slander.

1 PETER 2:1

What comes to mind when unbelievers think of Christians? Unfortunately, it's often the word *hypocrite*.

Hypocrisy comes from not living what we say we believe. We condemn certain sins, but then we commit similar sins ourselves. When we do that, we put a huge stumbling block in the paths of others who are watching us.

God calls us to transparency, not hypocrisy.

I don't know what today's Day One holds for you, but if you have a choice today between being open, transparent, and honest versus being a hypocrite, I hope you'll choose the former. If that means admitting you're not perfect (and none of us are), then go ahead and admit it. Most people will respect you for your honesty and for stepping out from behind the mask of hypocrisy.

Today Is **DAY ONE**

Finish Well

I do not account my life of any value nor as precious to myself, if only I may finish my course and the ministry that I received from the Lord Jesus, to testify to the gospel of the grace of God.

ACTS 20:24

I'm still young. At least in my eyes, I'm young. God is in charge of my future, but I have every hope of many productive years ahead of me. But whether my years be few or many, I want to arrive on my last day having lived well and finished well. A life with few regrets.

I know that if I'm going to arrive at that goal, I must start now. Being productive isn't a goal for tomorrow; it's a task for today. Finishing well *then* means living well *now*. That's why every single Day One is important. Our future depends on what we do today.

The problem is, we can easily fall into a dull routine of living day after day. Today is pretty much like yesterday, and tomorrow will be pretty much like today. That kind of thinking leads to a dull life and a forgetful finish.

Don't accept that for your life. Live well today. Give God glory. Give Him thanks. Do what you know to be His will on this Day One. Start planning to finish well now. Don't wait until tomorrow.

Fellowship

A friend loves at all times,
and a brother is born for adversity.

PROVERBS 17:17

I'm always excited when my Day One includes meeting with other believers. Sometimes that's on Sunday at church. Other times it's getting together with friends for a Bible study or just to talk and share our lives with one another. Good fellowship makes Day One richer. God created us for community, not for isolation.

Let me ask you this: What are your sources of fellowship? Are you part of a church that feeds you spiritually? Are you growing as you meet together with other believers? How about close friends? Do they know the Lord? Do you have someone you can share confidences with? Whom would you call if you desperately needed prayer right now?

What happens if you remove a burning log from the campfire and set it off by itself? It soon goes out, right? But as long as the log is kept in the fire pit with the other burning logs, it continues to burn brightly. That's a picture of us. We need to be in the fire pit, burning brightly and helping others to rekindle the fire in their hearts.

I hope on this Day One you'll seek out another believer or get together with some others in your church or fellowship. Talk together, share burdens, pray together, and worship the Lord. This is what you were meant for.

Today Is DAY ONE

The Answer

Now faith is confidence in what we hope for and assurance about what we do not see.

HEBREWS 11:1 NIV

Recently, American Pharaoh became the first horse in 37 years to win horseracing's coveted Triple Crown, winning the Kentucky Derby, Preakness Stakes, and Belmont Stakes.

Now, I'm not much of a racing fan. But with history in the making, I tuned in to see what the fuss was all about. As the horses lined up and prepared for the gates to open, a commentator said in a dramatic tone, "Will American Pharaoh win the Triple Crown? The answer is just a mile and a half away." His words drew me in, and I was glued to the television to watch American Pharaoh emerge victorious.

After I turned off the TV, that commentator's "mile and a half away" cliff-hanger stuck with me. Wouldn't it be nice to know when we'll receive the answers we seek in life? Of course, I prefer immediate answers to all of life's questions, but I'd settle for God at least giving me a little heads-up. *Hey, Matthew, you know that question you've been praying about lately? Well, the answer is coming up on Tuesday.*

But if we had access to God's timetable, life wouldn't require faith. And faith is what God requires of us. Faith that He will provide. Faith that He is in control. Faith to follow Him even when we don't know the outcome.

The answers to your unknowns might be just a mile and a half away, or they might be farther off. Ask God to give you faith in the meantime. He knows all things, sees all things, and will lead you to the answers you seek.

Why Do You Call Me Lord?

Why do you call me "Lord, Lord," and
not do what I tell you?

LUKE 6:46

I don't know about you, but I'm a busy man. It seems like I'm always on the go. And the things I do are good things. I try not to waste a lot of time. I don't have time to waste.

The problem with being busy is that it's easy to let some of the most important things slip by. To be honest, God is less concerned about my next concert being sold out than He is about people going to bed hungry only a mile from the arena.

When the day comes that we're standing before the Lord, it won't do any good to say, "Lord, I was too busy to help the poor or the sick or visit the prisoners." If we're too busy to do hands-on work for the Lord, we're just plain too busy. This isn't meant to lay a guilt trip on us. God isn't into motivation through guilt. He's into motivation through love.

I believe every Day One should include an acknowledgment of our Christian responsibility for the poor, the needy, the oppressed. If we don't love them, how can we say the love of God is in us?

That probably won't mean every Day One will see us calling on prisoners or taking food baskets to the hungry. But it does mean that if we're serious about our faith—if we're serious about making Day One relevant to God and to our faith—we'll be asking God how we can get involved in walking the walk that we call the gospel.

No guilt here. Just motivation to love and serve those whom God loves.

Not Just the Good Parts

We know that in all things God works for the good of those who love him, who have been called according to his purpose.

ROMANS 8:28 NIV

If you want God to use you, you must make the bold choice to place your whole story in His hands, not just the good parts. Then prepare to be blown away as He chooses to shine through some surprising chapters. It's not for us to pick and choose what God will use.

Most of us work hard to find out what we're good at, what sets us apart from the crowd, what special skills we have. Then we hone those abilities and show them off to the world. It's easy to see why we get fooled into thinking God's greatest work through us would come through our strengths.

I imagine myself lifting up my special skills to God and saying, "Here You go, God. Use my good stuff." What if all the while God is looking back and responding, "I know about your good stuff. I'm the One who gave it to you. Now, hand over all the rest. Give Me the worst mistake you've ever made and trust in My forgiveness once and for all. Give Me your hurts, your habits, and your hang-ups, and trust that I can use all of it for My glory."

The world doesn't need to see a perfectly polished version of you today. The world needs to see the authentically flawed version of you—someone whose broken pieces have been miraculously put together by the God who truly can work all things for the good.

Trust God with your whole story today. His perfect light shines best through imperfect people.

A Bottle for Your Tears

You have…put my tears in your bottle.
Are they not in your book?

PSALM 56:8

What happens when you start Day One but things don't go the way you want them to? You ask, *What's up with that, God? I didn't sign up for misery and heartbreak.*

Pain happens. Even during Day One.

Our pain can help us draw close to God. When we do, He draws close to us. He brings His bottle to catch our tears. When we cry as Christians, we never cry alone. God is always there. Not a tear falls that doesn't find its way into the bottle with our name on it.

One thing about pain and heartache—it doesn't come to stay. Tomorrow it may be gone. Or the day after. Or maybe next month. The point is that life is a journey, and there are bumps in the road to our destination. Once in a while, Day One will be a bumpy day. That's okay. Weather it with faith, knowing it will pass. Weather it in confidence, knowing that your bottle of fallen tears is precious to God.

Here Goes Nothin'

We can make our plans,
but the LORD determines our steps.

PROVERBS 16:9 NLT

A woman came up to me after a concert and said, "I just have to tell you that your song 'Day One' is my new theme song!" I asked her why that particular song was resonating with her. She responded, "'Cuz I just got fired from my job!" We laughed together, but I was impressed with her perspective.

Not knowing where her next paycheck would come from was scary, but she was excited to see where God would lead her next. Her favorite part of the song was the shout, "Here goes nothin'!"

I too have faced seasons when a door closed or a dream slipped out of reach. Perhaps you have as well. We will all have moments when life reminds us that it doesn't always share our opinion as to how things should go. These moments can push us in one of three directions: (1) We can stay focused on the door that just closed, hoping it will reopen (thus wasting time regretting the dream that didn't come true). (2) We can begin to doubt whether God is really in control of our life and begin taking matters in our own hands. (3) We can turn our back to the closed doors and trust that God is leading us in a new direction.

Moving into an unknown season of life is scary. But God is ultimately in control, and as today's Scripture says, He determines our steps. That truth can turn our fear of the unknown into a rush of excitement that will leave us waking up each morning following God's plan and singing, "Here goes nothin'!"

God's Way or My Way?

"I know the plans I have for you," declares the LORD, "plans to prosper you and not to harm you, plans to give you hope and a future."

JEREMIAH 29:11 NIV

The exciting thing about Day One is that God is in control. He has a plan, and He's working it out just fine without soliciting our advice. The best way to enjoy Day One is to discover His plan and join Him in working out what He wants to do. That means either altering our plans or tearing them up altogether.

So how do we know God's plan? Well, first we pray. Then we make sure our lives are aligned with His Word. Then we watch to see how God has arranged our circumstances. If we're still unsure, we can ask trusted fellow believers for advice.

From God's point of view, the journey ahead is clearly marked according to His divine plan. It gets complicated only when we look at our own road map and try to follow it to our destination, rather than trusting God's road map to His destination for us.

When you find yourself tempted to follow your own road map, remember that God's plan for you is "to prosper you and not to harm you." God's way promises hope and a future.

Good Deed for the Day

So let's not get tired of doing what is good. At just the right time we will reap a harvest of blessing if we don't give up.

GALATIANS 6:9 NLT

Early one morning, I was stumbling through an airport security line when I noticed a pilot and his crew waiting behind me. Their usual bypass through security was occupied at the moment. So I turned to the pilot and said, "Sir, you and your crew can go ahead of me." He thanked me, and they proceeded through security while I waited with my guitar. As I watched him go ahead, I thought to myself, *Well, that's my good deed for the day.*

And there it was—a moment of pride in myself for being so thoughtful. How ironic!

God calls us to more than just one good deed a day. Imagine if later that day I came across another person in need. Would it be okay for me to flash my "I already did a good deed" card and ignore the needy person? Of course not!

Each day brings us multiple opportunities to show the world a picture of kindness and love. Servanthood is a lifestyle, not a nine-to-five job. God's compassionate love for us has no limits, and His plan is for us to show that same compassion to the world.

Ask God to help you not get tired of doing what is good today. When you see the impact one act of kindness can have on someone, you'll be motivated to change the world with more than just one good deed for the day.

The Life of a Servant

[Jesus] sat down and called the twelve. And he said to them, "If anyone would be first, he must be last of all and servant of all."

MARK 9:35

We read about the disciples arguing about who was the greatest, and we laugh at their lack of humility. But really, aren't we the same way sometimes? When we raised our hand or walked down the aisle to accept Christ, did we realize what we were getting ourselves into? Did we know we were signing up to be servants? And not just servants of Jesus (who wouldn't want to serve *Him*?), but servants of all. Servants of our brothers and sisters in Christ, some of whom, truth be told, can be a bit demanding or ungrateful.

The truth—somewhat hidden from the world—is that having the heart of a servant is rewarding. There is more joy in serving than in being served. Jesus knew that. I think that's why He told us it's more blessed to give than to receive.

How would you feel about Day One if you knew that one of its essential elements is serving others? You'd feel great about it if you realized that being the lowest servant in God's kingdom brings more joy than being a king or queen on this earth.

Watch during this Day One and see if God provides you with an opportunity to serve. If so, jump at the chance. You're receiving an invitation to be a blessing and receive a blessing.

Today Is DAY ONE

A Ruined Cup of Coffee and a One-Way Conversation

My sheep hear my voice, and I know
them, and they follow me.
JOHN 10:27

This morning, I dropped my cell phone in a most unfortunate place—my cup of coffee.

It was unfortunate for two reasons. First, I ruined a perfectly good cup of local brew that I had just treated with cream and sugar. And second, the speaker of my phone no longer works. So I now have a phone that communicates only one way. I can talk all I want, but I can't hear anything coming back to me. Someone might be trying to say something, but I'm none the wiser. (Depending on the day, my wife might say our conversations work the same way my coffee-soaked phone does.)

Too many times, our talks with God are as one-sided as a conversation on a busted cell phone. The Bible promises us over and over again that God hears our prayers. But are we hearing God's voice? The key to healthy communication in any relationship isn't just talking but also listening.

In our communication with God, listening is just as essential as speaking. Don't settle for a one-sided conversation with your Creator today. He is listening. But He also wants you to hear His voice.

Killing Time

Look carefully then how you walk, not as unwise but as wise, making the best use of the time, because the days are evil. Therefore do not be foolish, but understand what the will of the Lord is.

EPHESIANS 5:15-17

This Day One offers you a one-of-a-kind opportunity to live for God. So what will you do with that opportunity?

One thing I hope you won't do—and I hope I won't either—is to think of some way to kill time. Ack. What a thought—considering time as something so valueless as to be killed.

I know it's just an expression, but we need to remember that time is precious, not disposable. Time is what life is made up of. If we kill time, we kill part of our life on earth. What would happen to our Day One if we began to treasure time? What if we "redeemed" the time? If we made the most of the hours given us here on earth? One thing is certain—once time is gone, it's irretrievable. If we lose money, we can earn more. If we lose our health, that too can be recovered. A lost job can be replaced by a new one. But time, once spent, is forever gone.

Let's not settle for killing time on this Day One. Let's live each momet mindful that each moment matters and we only live each moment once.

Today Is

DAY ONE

Jesus Knows Me, This I Love

You have searched me, LORD, and you know me. You know when I sit and when I rise; you perceive my thoughts from afar. You discern my going out and my lying down; you are familiar with all my ways. Before a word is on my tongue you, LORD, know it completely.

PSALM 139:1-4 NIV

I saw it scribbled in purple ink, lying on the nightstand next to my six-year-old daughter Delaney's bed. A sheet of paper, torn from the Hello Kitty journal she convinced either her mom or me to buy her on our most recent trip to the mall. What I read on that sheet of paper stopped me in my tracks. "Jesus knows me, this I love."

At first I thought to myself, *How cute—she got the words to the song mixed up.* But as I picked up that piece of paper and read it again, I was struck by what a wonderful word scramble she had pieced together. We sing mostly of Jesus's love for us. But to be truly loved means to be fully known. And we are known by our Creator.

The Author of all history is penning every sentence of your story. The great I Am knows who you are. The Alpha and Omega, the beginning and the end, has known you from your beginning and will walk with you to the end.

Spend a few moments thanking God today for knowing every detail of your life—the good, the bad, the ugly—and loving you still.

To be fully known is to be fully loved.

With My *Whole* Heart?

I will give thanks to the LORD with my whole heart.

PSALM 9:1

It will come as no surprise that on a hard day, it's not easy for me to give thanks with my whole heart. Half my heart, maybe, but my *whole* heart? When I just burned up the engine in my car? When the tests came back positive for cancer? When the bank says I'm overdrawn? When my spouse and I are at odds?

And yet the psalmist's admonition—and God's will—is for us to give thanks with our whole heart.

I think I've figured out why God wants us to do this. If God is God, then He is never surprised by what happens to us. He never says, "Wow, I didn't see that coming your way!" When we thank God with our whole heart, even in dire circumstances, we are saying, "Okay, this thing has happened to me and I hate it, but I know my God is bigger than this situation."

He is the God who controls all things, and He sees the end from the beginning. We see only the present trouble, but God sees the end. He knows we will get through this. Giving thanks with our whole heart is our way of letting go of stress. We stop wondering what to do next, and we trust God for the outcome.

It's easy to give thanks when all is well. It's when we hit a rough patch that we need to show our faith by giving thanks with our whole heart to the One who sees the blessed end of every difficult situation.

Today Is

DAY ONE

Be Present in God's Presence

[Jesus] returned and found the disciples asleep. He said to Peter, "Simon, are you asleep? Couldn't you watch with me even one hour?"

MARK 14:37 NLT

There will never be a shortage of distractions when we make up our minds to spend time with God. I wake up in the morning with a desire to spend some much-needed time reading my Bible and writing in my prayer journal, only to be hit with a barrage of items fighting for my attention. So many thoughts, concerns, things to do, problems to solve. Before I know it, my focus has shifted from God to these other things, and distraction steals me away from where I need to be.

Perhaps you can relate? If so, be encouraged knowing you and I are not the only ones. Even Jesus's disciples had a hard time in the Garden of Gethsemane. Jesus took them with Him while He went to pray. And when Jesus had finished praying, did He return to find the disciples deep in prayer, crying out to God?

No, they were asleep. Probably sawing logs on the outskirts of the garden. Did Jesus give up on them? No, He loved them despite their inability to stay awake. In fact, He had declared that Peter, one of the slumbering disciples, was the rock upon which He would build His church (Matthew 16:18).

When distractions come, don't get discouraged. God knows we're prone to wander. Just whisper a prayer and ask Him to quiet the distractions. His voice will cut through the clutter and reward you for your efforts to be with Him.

DAY ONE

Jesus, Friend of Sinners

The Son of Man has come eating and drinking, and you say, "Look at him! A glutton and a drunkard, a friend of tax collectors and sinners!" Yet wisdom is justified by all her children.

LUKE 7:34-35

I love knowing that Jesus was (and is!) the friend of sinners. The Pharisees couldn't handle that. They thought their righteousness, based on trying to keep the Law, made them God's friends. They wouldn't dare hang with gluttons, drunkards, tax collectors...*sinners*.

But what was Jesus's mission on earth? He tells us in Luke 19:10, "The Son of Man came to seek and to save the lost."

In order to be found, you must first know you're lost. The self-righteous have no sense of being lost. Their self-righteousness prevents them from seeing their true spiritual state.

Those who are caught up in sin and its deceitfulness know they are lost. They know they need a righteousness that doesn't come from their own efforts, for their own efforts always fall short. Their only hope is in a savior—and Jesus is that Savior.

Of course, "they," "those," "them"...it's really *me*, and presumably you too. We are the sinners Jesus came to save. The day we realize that is our true Day One. And every day after that can be a new Day One of realizing how lost we are without Christ and how very, very found we are with Him.

Today Is
DAY ONE

Finish the Race

I have fought the good fight, I have finished the race, I have kept the faith.

2 TIMOTHY 4:7 NIV

A University of Oregon distance runner recently lost a race in a most embarrassing fashion. He had the race won by a mile, you could say. But as he entered the final stretch, thinking none of the other runners were even close, he began celebrating his victory. He raised his arms in the air and waved to the crowd, and as a result, he slowed down. He began his victory lap before even crossing the finish line. A University of Washington runner saw the premature celebration and seized the opportunity to gain some ground. He passed the would-be champion and won the race by inches. The losing runner lay on his back on the track with his head in his hands in utter disbelief.

The story reminds me of Paul's final letter to Timothy. "I have fought the good fight, I have finished the race, I have kept the faith." Notice that he doesn't say he won the good fight, only that he fought it. Likewise, he doesn't tell Timothy he won the race, only that he finished it.

Paul was on the final lap of the race of his life, and instead of making it a victory lap, he was finishing strong with humility and honesty, sending you and me the message that we are not called to win this life's race but to finish it. There is no victory lap promised to us in this life, but those who keep the faith will receive the prize of heaven. "I press on toward the goal to win the prize for which God has called me heavenward in Christ Jesus" (Philippians 3:14 NIV).

Seeds

A sower went out to sow. And as he sowed, some seeds fell along the path, and the birds came and devoured them. Other seeds fell on rocky ground, where they did not have much soil, and immediately they sprang up, since they had no depth of soil, but when the sun rose they were scorched. And since they had no root, they withered away. Other seeds fell among thorns, and the thorns grew up and choked them. Other seeds fell on good soil and produced grain, some a hundredfold, some sixty, some thirty. He who has ears, let him hear.

MATTHEW 13:3-9

I like to think of every Day One as a day of planting seeds. If you've ever had a garden, you understand Jesus's point in the verses above.

Not all the seeds we plant will grow. Some get lost, some don't find fertile ground, some get eaten by the birds. But some of the seeds do sprout, grow, and bear fruit.

Some of what you do today really won't matter much in the big scheme of things. Some tasks will be like lost seeds that for one reason or another never sprout.

But you never know what God will do with the seeds you sow. However, you do know God wants you to reap a good crop from the seeds you sow. Here's the secret: Keep sowing seeds every Day One, and in faith, leave the rest to God. He can bless the seeds you sow, but you do have to sow them.

Be aware of sowing seeds today. Look for ways to plant seeds God can bless. Then leave the rest to Him.

Today Is DAY ONE

Keep Your Head Up

I'm not trying to win the approval of people, but of God.
GALATIANS 1:10 NLT

Comparing yourself to others sets your feet on a path to one destination—a life of discontent. I can say this with great authority because I have foolishly traveled the path of comparison countless times. *Why does he have a nicer house than me? How come she got the promotion? Why didn't they invite us to the party?* The comparison game is a losing one every single time. It is also a telltale sign that my focus is on winning the approval of others instead of God.

How can we take our focus off others? Some people say, "Just keep your head down." That fixes half of the problem. By keeping my head down, I can move forward in my life without comparing my success to those around me. But keeping my head down also turns my focus inward, as if it were up to me to become the best version of myself. Then, if I reach a certain goal or milestone in life, my tendency is to think I'm responsible for my success.

Instead of looking down or looking around, keep your head up. The world is focused on making sure that everybody measures up to everybody else. Don't waste Day One on this path to discontent. Seek the approval of the One who never compares you to anyone else—He created you just the way you are. In God's eyes, you are beyond compare. So lift your eyes, keep your head up, and bask in the glow of a love that is beyond compare.

DAY ONE

A Redeemed Past

As far as the east is from the west,
so far does he remove our transgressions from us.

PSALM 103:12

A s I read the Bible, I'm amazed by the number of people of faith who had questionable pasts. Abraham, Moses, Rahab, Jacob, Mary Magdalene, Peter (who denied the Lord)...Do you have a questionable past? Perhaps you've been discouraged thinking God can't use you because of something you've done?

The good news is, that's far from true. And it's not just that God overlooks our past or that we're free from condemnation because Jesus paid for our sins. As fantastic and wonderful as that is, the truth is that our past is so far removed from us that God can, if necessary, use that past as a building block for our future.

Every Day One is proof that whatever is in our past (even if we failed yesterday), God is able to redeem it. Don't let the enemy rob you of your future by holding it hostage to your past.

Thank God on this Day One for your redeemed past.

Today Is **DAY ONE**

Subject to Change

Since we are living by the Spirit,
let us follow the Spirit's leading in every part of our lives.
GALATIANS 5:25 NLT

Does your to-do list leave any room for the Spirit's leading today? Nothing is wrong with making plans, setting goals, and dreaming dreams. God has created us to think, dream, and do amazing things. But He also wants full control of those thoughts, goals, and dreams. The plans we make should always include a determined disclaimer: "Subject to change."

Last year on July 4, my family and I made plans to watch fireworks. But it rained all evening, and guess what the town's website said about the fireworks display? "Subject to change." No fair. No fun! But you know what happened? The sun came out on July 5, and we had an amazing time watching the fireworks a day late. What would have happened if we had ignored the message that the fireworks were postponed and showed up for them anyway? It would have literally rained on our parade. But we were forced to go with the flow and trust that when the time was right, we'd get to see those fireworks. And we did.

Take a few moments today to hold your to-do list up to the light. Share your plans, goals, and dreams with God in the form of a question. *Lord, this is what's on my heart today. Is this in line with what You have planned for me, or is there something else You want for me?*

When you leave room for God to make changes, you can know His changes will always be for the better and will lead you into the fulfilling life He has planned for you.

Whatever You Do

Whatever you do, work heartily, as
for the Lord and not for men.

Colossians 3:23

I love the word *whatever*. That brings God—our heavenly Father—into every aspect of our life. He's not just for Sunday morning or midweek Bible study. He's in my music, He's in my family life, He's in my reading, He's in my hobbies—He's in *all* my life.

When we think about Day One—today and every day—we don't have to divide our day into segments and invite God into some of them. No, God is in *whatever* we do, and as a result, we can see His power manifested throughout our day.

Have you read *The Practice of the Presence of God* by Brother Lawrence? He was a monk in the Middle Ages who served his monastery by working in the kitchen. While washing dishes and going about his "whatever," he was able to experience God's presence. Yes, even in the dull routine of washing dishes.

I don't know what your "whatever" will be today, but I hope it includes the Lord. Make Him part of every aspect of your Day One.

Today Is
DAY ONE

Not So Light and Momentary

Our light and momentary troubles are achieving for us
an eternal glory that far outweighs them all.
2 Corinthians 4:17 niv

Sometimes our troubles feel anything but "light and momentary." As a matter of fact, the trials in my daily life often feel heavy and never-ending. But I love how the apostle Paul shifts the way we view our troubles by comparing them to the reward that awaits us—"an eternal glory." Paul was no stranger to trouble. Persecution, prison, hardships...all just another day at the office for him. Yet he wasn't focused on himself or his circumstances. His focus was on Christ and the eternal reward of heaven.

Have you noticed the ways people try to shift their focus and make their problems seem more bearable? Some people set their sights on the upcoming weekend. Some count down the days until their beach vacation. Some dream of retirement. I mean, how else can someone cope? But the only way to shift your focus and view your problems as "light and momentary" is the one that Paul encourages—by looking to eternity.

In light of the upcoming weekend, our problems still loom large. As for a vacation, we know that when it ends, we'll have to dust the sand off our feet and travel back to our reality. We may even reach retirement only to realize that we still reside in a broken world with no shortage of problems. But in the light of the promise that we will get to spend eternity far away from the troubles of this life...well, those troubles can't help but grow strangely dim as the future looks brighter and brighter every day.

Today Is
DAY ONE

I Owe You

He who did not spare his own Son, but gave him up for us all—how will he not also, along with him, graciously give us all things?

ROMANS 8:32 NIV

Recently, I took my family out for dinner. Once we arrived and had ordered, I discovered that we were dining at the last restaurant on earth that won't accept credit cards. "CASH ONLY," the sign read. I knew I was going to come up a bit short because I didn't carry much cash. That's when I noticed my daughter's sparkly purple purse sitting on our table. I knew there was some cash in that purse because I had given it to her.

Sure enough, the check came, and I came up short.

"Lulu, can I borrow two dollars?" I asked.

Lulu responded, "Sure, but you owe me!" As you can imagine, Lulu didn't stop reminding me about the money I owed her until I paid her back. Can you see the irony? I'm the one who gave her that two dollars in the first place. I'm the one who bought the purple purse that held the two dollars. I'm the one who paid for her dinner that required her two dollars! You get the idea. As parents we provide for our children—it's what we do. So the thought of still owing my daughter two dollars cracked me up!

This is how I treat God sometimes. Everything I have is a gift from Him. Yet my prayers sometimes sound as if they're coming from a heart that has forgotten this. I pray as if God owes me something when God owes me nothing.

Look around your life today and be reminded that every gift has come from the same source. We are the ones who owe Him everything. Yet all He asks is that you live for Him on this Day One.

Today Is
DAY ONE

Power in Weakness

My grace is all you need. My power works best in weakness.

2 Corinthians 12:9 NLT

Patricia's voice was soft and shaking, and she had tears in her eyes as she approached me after a concert. The reason her voice was soft? Thyroid cancer. She had been diagnosed a few years ago and had undergone surgery. Today she's a cancer survivor, but the surgery left her vocal chords paralyzed, and for two years she had no voice at all.

Patricia said she had read my story about my own season of silence. In 2007, I had career-threatening vocal cord surgery. She said she found encouragement knowing someone else had gone through a similar trial. She watched a documentary I made called *Nothing to Say* that chronicled my journey of surgery and recovery, and she remembered the scenes that showed me trying to communicate with a dry-erase board. She remembered one question I scribbled on the board—"Will I ever get my voice back?" She had asked herself the same question for two years.

As she told me her story, I was reminded of the powerful ways God uses our lives, even in our weaknesses. In the middle of my own trial, the last thing on my mind was the notion that God could use this season of silence to help somebody else.

My voice came back, and Patricia's did too. Hers isn't as strong as it once was, at times barely above a whisper. But in a way, it's stronger than ever. She is now a teacher at a correctional facility, helping inmates prepare for life after incarceration.

Let Patricia's story remind you that God can speak through our lives in more ways than just our voices. In our weakness, His power is on display.

Today Is DAY ONE

Why Is It Taking So Looong?

I am weary with my crying out; my throat is parched.
My eyes grow dim with waiting for my God.
PSALM 69:3

Are you in a waiting mode right now? Maybe you're not where you want to be, and it seems as if God is taking forever to move you ahead.

Why does God sometimes seem to take so long to bring desired change to our lives? All I can suggest is that we're meant to be like slow-growing oak trees. They seem to take forever to become mature. Other plants—particularly weeds—spring up practically overnight and grow faster than we can pull them up. But then, we're not weeds. We're way more than that. God takes time—lots of time—with the kinds of trees that are durable, meant to last through wind and storm.

If an oak tree could talk, I don't think it would complain about God being slow. It would remind us that when God seems to be slow to move, it's by His design and for reasons we wouldn't understand. It would tell us to trust our Creator, not to doubt Him.

If this Day One is filled with longing for what will come next, turn that longing into a prayer and thank God for working with you at His speed, not yours. After all, He knows better than you do how to grow an oak.

Stay Awhile

My presence will go with you, and I will give you rest.
Exodus 33:14

Stay in God's presence long enough to listen. Sometimes I devote just enough time to read my laundry list of things I need God to do for me before I begin to wrap up my prayer time and dive headfirst into my busy day. Sometimes as I utter my "Amen," I feel as if my heart hears the whisper of my Savior saying, *Stay awhile, Matthew. Don't go so soon. Rest in My presence. I have what you will need to face the rest of the day.*

I once had the honor of meeting Billy Graham at his home in the hills of North Carolina. I will not soon forget the experience of sitting at his kitchen table, drinking root beer (his favorite treat), and talking about ministry. One of the things he said really stuck with me. He looked me in the eye and said, "The quality of your family, your ministry, and your whole life depends on the quality of your time spent alone with God."

Those words were spoken from a man who learned that lesson firsthand. When I do answer God's invitation to linger in His presence, I'm always so glad I listened. What's more, I find that the more time I spend in God's presence, allowing Him to pour into my life, the more tuned in to His presence I remain throughout my day.

When was the last time you actually lost track of time while praying because you were enjoying such a rich experience in God's presence? Has it been a while? If so, then maybe today is Day One of accepting His invitation to stay awhile.

Hard Days

A windstorm came down on the lake, and they were filling with water and were in danger. And they went and woke [Jesus], saying, "Master, Master, we are perishing!" And he awoke and rebuked the wind and the raging waves, and they ceased, and there was a calm. He said to them, "Where is your faith?"

LUKE 8:23-25

I love it when each Day One goes well. Everything moves along like clockwork. Smooth sailing all the way.

But let's be real. Not every Day One will be like that. Some days there will be rough waters to navigate. God's promise is to be with us in the storms of life, to help us navigate them—not to eliminate them.

I hope this Day One is everything you want it to be. I hope the sea is calm for you. But if that doesn't happen, hold tight to God and wait out the storm. He's there with you—rely on that. Accept hard days with stamina, just as you accept happy days with joy.

Every Day One that you commit to the Lord will turn out right—even if you don't see the results right away. Your storm is under God's control. Your hard day is God's unfinished story.

Tired of Throwing Pennies in a Well?

If the Son sets you free, you will be free indeed.
JOHN 8:36

How many pennies have you thrown in a well? How many times have you thought to yourself, *I wish I could quit doing this*, or *I wish I could change this about how I'm living*?

Like most people, I have many childhood memories of being dragged to the shopping mall against my will. I used to fantasize about how much money was at the bottom of that fountain in the middle of the mall, and I devised a plan to one day scoop up that sunken treasure while no one was looking.

But here's the treasure God has offered us right now, today: You don't have to wish for change. You *are* changed. "If the Son sets you free, you will be free indeed." If you have fully committed your whole life to Christ, He is fully committed to change you from the inside out and make you more like Him.

His power dwells within you. His power can change you from who you were to who He created you to be. Don't waste your time simply wishing you could change this or that about yourself. Turn your wish into this daily prayer: *Lord, I have given my life to You completely. You know everything about me. I believe I am "free indeed," and I ask You to keep changing me and making me more like You.*

Pop Quiz

Be ready in season and out of season.
2 TIMOTHY 4:2

Did your teachers ever hand out pop quizzes? You'd arrive at school expecting a normal day with little or no stress, and out of nowhere a teacher would announce a pop quiz. You had to be caught up on your studies or you'd fail the quiz.

Sometimes if we're not walking in faith toward God, an event will come up that will seem like a pop quiz. We need to make a decision—and it better be the right decision or we'll suffer the consequences.

Any student can be prepared for an announced test. During finals week, you expect final exams, so you're ready for them. But who can be ready for a pop quiz? Only those who have kept up with the assigned work and haven't gone slack in their homework.

Likewise, we can pass any of life's pop quizzes if we haven't slacked off in our walk with God. We're ready in season and out of season. During finals week and on pop quiz day.

On this Day One, you may have a pop quiz. If so, don't panic. Stay focused on what you know. Do the right thing and trust God, and you'll pass with flying colors.

Worry Won't Add Up

Who of you by worrying can add a single hour to your life?
LUKE 12:25 NIV

If state fairs held "best worrier" contests, I would be the champion. Come to think of it, I'd probably worry too much about how the competition would go. Then I would worry about what to wear. Then I would probably worry about what kind of food they would have at the competition and whether I would have an allergic reaction to something. Then I would worry about what would happen if I won the competition and had to give an acceptance speech, which would lead to me worrying that I might forget to thank the right people who have made me the worrier I am today.

All that worry would probably prevent me from even signing up for the worry competition! Whew, I'm exhausted already from all this worry talk.

And isn't worry just that? Worry is an exhausting, draining, and useless waste of time that does nothing to change our circumstances. So let's not go there today. Let's refuse to sign up for that worry competition. When worry tries to occupy your thoughts today, revisit Luke's reminder that worrying can't add a single hour to your life.

And consider this. While worrying won't add a single hour to your life, choosing *not* to worry will multiply your time of focusing your thoughts on the positive truth that God is completely in control of your life today.

Why Me, Lord?

I give you thanks, O Lᴏʀᴅ, with my whole heart;
before the gods I sing your praise;
I bow down toward your holy temple
 and give thanks to your name for your steadfast love
and your faithfulness,
 for you have exalted above all things
your name and your word.

Psᴀʟᴍ 138:1-2

Usually when we ask, *Why me, Lord?* we're wondering why God allowed some bad thing in our life. On this Day One, let's turn that around. Regardless of what happens today, let's resolve to ask God, *Why me, Lord?* about all the good in our life.

Have you thought about that lately? God is good to us. He's given us blessings we often take for granted. Sure, stuff happens we wish wouldn't happen. But let's focus on the many good things God has brought into our lives.

It shouldn't take long to come up with a good list.

Start with, *Wow, God, I'm still alive on planet earth! Why me, Lord?* From there, add your own blessings. How about your job? Your family? Your relationships? Your church? Your salvation? Your heavenly home in eternity?

Give God praise on this Day One and ask Him, *Why me, Lord?* about all the good you see in your life.

Dash

What is your life? For you are a mist that appears for a little time and then vanishes.

JAMES 4:14

When we look at a gravestone, we typically focus on two things—the date someone was born and the date they died. We don't really notice the little dash between the two numbers. That dash is the life someone lived, a tiny little mark representing a person's time on earth from beginning to end. That dash is all we get—and we are living our dash right now.

The Bible's reminders of the brevity of life aren't intended to frighten us. They provide much-needed perspective so we won't waste the little time we're given on useless worrying or aimless endeavors.

Scripture also doesn't say, "Life is short. Good luck." No, the Bible is a blueprint for how to make the most of our dash. God's plan for your life is for you to live in such a way that the dash extends beyond the numbers. Oh, you won't see it on a gravestone, but it will be there. A life fully devoted to Jesus creates a dash that goes beyond the numbers on a chunk of granite. God is calling each of us to leave a pathway for others to follow and to secure an eternity in heaven at the end of our time on earth.

Draw a little dash in your journal or on a sheet of paper and place it somewhere you will see it. Let it challenge you to make the most of your life, and let it remind you that you're a dash, a mist, a flower quickly fading. But you're here on this earth right now for a reason. Seek the One who knows that reason, and your dash will go far beyond the numbers.

The Best Offense

The LORD is my strength and my shield;
in him my heart trusts, and I am helped;
my heart exults, and with my song I give thanks to him.

PSALM 28:7

I'm sure you've heard the saying "The best defense is a good offense." Well, the psalmist who wrote this verse in Psalm 28 seemed to have an understanding that God provides us with both offense and defense to face the world each day.

"The LORD is my strength and my *shield*." A shield is someone or something that provides protection. When I think of a shield, I get an instant picture of the movie *Gladiator* and the epic scenes in the Colosseum. In one particular scene, the slaves who were thrown into battle realized the power of their shields as they all huddled together, shields out, causing one of the royal chariots to topple over in defeat.

God is your source of strength to make it through this Day One. He is also your shield—the provider of protection from everything that life will throw at you. In other words, He's got you covered. On all sides.

When the warriors in the Colosseum joined together and used their shields to protect each other, their confidence grew as they went on the offensive and claimed victory for the day. You may never know in this life all the things that God has shielded you from. But you can rise up and face this Day One with confidence that as long as you put your trust in Him, strength and protection will always surround you.

More Than One Day One

"Now come and have some breakfast!" Jesus said.
None of the disciples dared to ask him, "Who
are you?" They knew it was the Lord.

JOHN 21:12 NLT

For Peter, every day had been pretty much the same. Same boat, same brothers, same nets, same water, same fish. But from the day Jesus called out to him, Peter's life would never be the same. "And he said to them, 'Follow me, and I will make you fishers of men'" (Matthew 4:19).

This was Day One of Peter's new life following Christ. And the Bible says Peter and the others never hesitated when they heard Jesus's invitation. Matter of fact, Peter never seemed to hesitate even after he traded in his nets. When Jesus was arrested, Peter was quick to defend his Master by grabbing a sword and slicing off a guard's ear (John 18:10). Later, impetuous Peter didn't hesitate to deny that he even knew the One he once defended (John 18:17,25-27). And after Jesus was crucified, Peter didn't hesitate to return back to his old life, saying, "I am going fishing" (John 21:3).

Yes, Peter had failed. He knew it. His first Day One of following Jesus must have felt a million years ago. But Jesus, risen from the dead, refused to give up on Peter and knew where to find him. When Peter saw the Lord, he again acted without hesitation (see John 21:7 NLT).

Jesus was reaching out to Peter, not to judge him for the ways he had failed, but to offer him a new start. Peter responded with no hesitation. Jesus is reaching out to you too, today. Take a cue from Peter and respond with no hesitation by jumping into your new beginning today.

Shine!

Let your light shine before others, so that they may see your good works and give glory to your Father who is in heaven.

Matthew 5:16

Darkness is increasing in the world every day. But as the world gets darker, the light shines brighter. That's where you and I come in. We're called to be light in a dark world.

So how do we do that? Lots of ways. We shine by doing good when we can. We shine by feeding the hungry when we can, visiting prisoners, and taking care of the sick. We shine by acknowledging God as our source of light and by pointing others to Him. We shine by simply being honest, ethical, and kind to others. We shine by doing what God has called us to do. I try to shine as I'm faithful to my musical calling. You will shine in your own unique way.

The important thing about shining is that we give glory to our Father who is in heaven. In other words, we don't shine to call attention to ourselves. We shine for God.

Today is your Day One. Go shine God's glory wherever you go and whatever you do.

Follow Me

You follow me!

JOHN 21:22

Poor Peter. He got it wrong so many times. At the transfiguration, he was at a loss for words, so he blurted out, "Uh...let's make three tabernacles!" On the Sea of Galilee, he took a few steps on the water but then took his eyes off Jesus and started sinking. Shortly before the crucifixion, he denied even knowing the Lord. And after the resurrection, we see him sticking his nose in other people's business. "When Peter saw [John], he said to Jesus, 'Lord, what about this man?'" Jesus didn't mince words: "What is that to you? You follow me!"

And so he did. Peter and John both had faith-filled adventures serving the Lord. Peter, as the story goes, was martyred for his faith, while John lived to a ripe old age and presumably died a natural death.

Do you look around at what others are doing and ask the Lord, "But what about him? What about her?" I think Jesus would give you the same reply He gave Peter. "You follow me!"

If you set aside expectations and comparisons with others, you'll find your own life of faith—the life God has envisioned for you. Not the one for your friend at church. Or your sibling. Or me. Or anyone else.

God's plan for you is just for you. On this Day One, just follow Jesus. It will be enough.

Every Good and Perfect Gift

Every good and perfect gift is from above, coming down from the Father of the heavenly lights, who does not change like shifting shadows.

JAMES 1:17 NIV

I remember singing these words as a child in church: "Count your blessings, name them one by one; count your blessings, see what God hath done!"

As an adult, I've found that when I live out these words, taking time each day to literally count my blessings, I forget to count my troubles.

One of the most powerful ways to radically change our outlook on life is to shift our focus from grumbling to gratitude.

I love the way James 1:17 reminds us where our blessings come from and then describes God as "the Father of the heavenly lights." When we make the conscious choice to count our blessings and recognize they are gifts from the Father of heavenly lights, we lose count of our worries. We also begin to see our trials in a new light—God's heavenly light.

Let the reminder of God's blessings, His faithfulness, and His unchanging goodness help you greet your current circumstances with confidence. Whatever looks like anything but a "good and perfect gift" is actually a blessing in the making. As your life continues to unfold, the trials along the way will eventually become items on your list of blessings.

God Knows

Nothing is hidden that will not be made manifest,
 nor is anything secret that will not be
 known and come to light.

Luke 8:17

I suspect everyone has secrets they're afraid someone will find out. If they became public, we'd be horrified, embarrassed, and shamed.

But God knows every one of our secrets. We can keep secrets from everyone but Him. And that's a good thing. We desperately need someone who knows our secrets—and who better than the One who created us, knows us the most intimately, and best of all, loves us the most.

Even so, many of us harbor our secrets from God. We do this by not opening up to Him about our secrets. By opening up, I mean talking to Him about them. God hears our every word directed to Him, and I suspect He hears our pains, pleas, and secrets most of all.

I wonder if God gave us secrets for that very reason—so we would be prompted to come to Him more often and open up with our secrets. When we do that, we open ourselves to healing, consolation, and wisdom about what to do with our secrets. After all, some secrets should no longer be hidden. Some secrets should be told to the right person.

The great thing about Day One is that it's a time to begin again. Today if you have secrets God needs to hear, open up to Him. Let Him take the burden of secrets off your shoulders. And if you know you should be telling someone else about one or more of your secrets, pray for God to show you who that person is...and then follow through by setting aside time with that person for a private talk.

In Any and Every Situation

I can do all things through him who gives me strength.
PHILIPPIANS 4:13 NIV

I used to think Philippians 4:13 applied to eleventh-hour whispered prayers before Little League baseball games and final exams. I would quote it under my breath before stepping up to bat in the late innings of a tie game or as I stepped into a classroom unprepared for a test.

I just knew that verse meant God would give me supernatural strength to knock one out of the park or eke out a passing grade on the test. I've grown out of that baseball uniform, but I've grown into a true understanding of God's strength and my daily need for it. In the preceding verse the apostle Paul writes, "I know what it is to be in need, and I know what it is to have plenty. I have learned the secret of being content in any and every situation, whether well fed or hungry, whether living in plenty or in want."

Paul knew he needed God's strength "in any and every situation."

On good days we can pray for His strength to live with a thankful attitude and a generous heart. On bad days we can cling to that same strength to put one foot in front of the other and walk in faith. God's strength is not a "get me out of a jam once in a while" kind of power.

If you're not mindful, life can lull you into a steady state of self-reliance. Be reminded today that you're simply not strong enough to make it through this life on your own. The great news is, you don't have to be. God's strength is available to you in any and every situation.

Overwhelmed

When I am overwhelmed,
you alone know the way I should turn.

PSALM 142:3 NLT

Can you think of a time when you felt totally overwhelmed by your circumstances? Perhaps you feel overwhelmed right now, in this very season of your life. The feeling of being overwhelmed by life can cause various physical and emotional responses. Some people struggle with extreme, life-gripping anxiety that leaves them frozen in fear. Some quickly rush in and try to take control of a situation, making hasty decisions they will later regret.

When I get overwhelmed, I tend to shut down. Sometimes I have felt so buried beneath layers and layers of problems that I just wanted to go to my bedroom, turn off the lights, shut the curtains and the door, and hide my head under the pillow instead of dealing with my emotions.

My eyes widened as I first came across this Scripture from Psalm 142. Notice—the word *when* implies that we will certainly feel overwhelmed on occasion. It's not a question of *if*; it's a question of *when*. We all get overwhelmed. It's inevitable in this crazy world in which we live. And when you do feel overwhelmed, make no mistake who will be there to help. "You alone know the way I should turn."

Commit this simple yet profound Scripture to memory, and the next time you feel overwhelmed, inhale a deep breath and exhale these words: "When I am overwhelmed, you alone know the way I should turn."

Find rest and peace in God's presence today.

Today Is DAY ONE

The Best Thing That Never Happened

This is the confidence we have in approaching God:
that if we ask anything according to his will, he hears us.

1 John 5:14 NIV

We tend to remember most fondly the best things that happen to us. But lately I've grown in my appreciation of the best things that never happened. Let me explain.

Growing up, I had my heart set on one goal—to be a professional baseball player. In high school I dreamed of the day I would receive a college scholarship to play baseball or a call from the big leagues. But during my senior season, I realized that dream wasn't going to come true. The scholarships never came. The phone never rang.

At about the same time, my parents began to encourage me to ask God about His plan for my life and to trust that His dreams were bigger than mine. Here's a shocker—Mom and Dad were right! They knew what they were talking about. I look at where I am now and smile because I'm so very glad my dream didn't come true. That baseball dream was the best thing that never happened. When that door closed, I learned that I'm here for a greater purpose and that God has a greater dream for me than I ever imagined.

The Bible is filled with promises that God will supply all our needs, that He will give us what we want. But ultimately, God knows what we really need and even what we really want. Today, seek Him and His will for your life. Do this, and you can be confident He will lead you where you will be most fulfilled in life. And you too will look back and smile about the best things that never happened in your life.

Alone with God

He said to them, "When you pray…"
LUKE 11:2

Do you ever get fidgety during your prayer time? You might rattle off a few prayers, then get quiet, and then look at your watch and think, *Wow. Two whole minutes praying. That'll do.*

Many of us have trouble focusing when we pray—and that's no sin. But we really shouldn't want to stay that way. We should be wanting a vibrant and spiritually satisfying time alone with God every day.

How does that happen? We need to really get it that God loves us and wants to be with us. We're not boring God by praying. We're actually engaged with Him, the Creator of the universe.

Here are some tips that have enriched my time with the Lord. Set aside a specific time to be alone with God and keep that appointment. (It may be short at first, but perhaps in time you'll enjoy it so much you'll make the appointment longer.) Start by worshipping God in your own words. Or maybe read a psalm or a New Testament Scripture. Think about what you've read and try turning it into a prayer. Then be thankful for what God's given you. Open your heart with gratitude. Share your secrets with God. Ask God to meet your deepest needs. Ask Him to direct your steps on this Day One. Close with another word of thanksgiving, and then take God with you as you joyfully go about your day. He's there with you.

Every Hair on Your Head

Even the hairs of your head are all numbered.

LUKE 12:7

God knows you. Like, really, really knows you. Every single detail of your life and every hair on your head. Does the thought that God is aware of everything about your life fill you with fear, amazement, or both?

Psalm 139 is a powerful poetic reminder of God's inescapable presence and His acute awareness of our lives. The psalmist wrote with a sense of wonder that the Creator of the universe was actually mindful of him. "You have searched me, LORD, and you know me" (Psalm 139:1 NIV). The writer later revisits the thought of God searching him, but this time in the form of a request. "Search me, God, and know my heart; test me and know my anxious thoughts. See if there is any offensive way in me, and lead me in the way everlasting" (verses 23-24 NIV).

Instead of being afraid of what God might find if He were to conduct a search of our hearts and lives, we can pray right along with the psalmist with confidence. God sees everything about us, and He isn't walking away, He isn't giving up on us. On the contrary, He loves us and wants to lead us in a new direction.

May the reminder that God searches and knows you entice you to ask Him to do so even more. And as you spend time in His presence, ask Him to reveal any "offensive way" in you so He can lead you into a better version of you. All the while, be thankful that the God who searches and knows you is the same God who stays and leads you.

No Fine Print

Ask, and it will be given to you; seek, and you
will find; knock, and it will be opened to you.
MATTHEW 7:7

Have you ever been burned by the fine print when signing a contract of some kind? Maybe you thought your car warranty covered the engine trouble you were having, but you were disappointed to get a bill because the fine print ruled out that particular part of the car. Or maybe you heard an advertisement on television or radio for a sweepstakes with an amazing grand prize, but at the very end of the ad you hear a voice speaking so fast that all you can make out is, "Some rules and restrictions may apply."

You don't have to look around this world too long to see how some things are not as good as they might appear. Oscar Wilde wrote, "The truth is rarely pure and never simple." In terms of this world we walk through, Oscar hit the nail on the head. But when it comes to God and His promises to us through Scripture, Mr. Wilde was dead wrong.

There is no fine print to trip us up in Matthew 7:7—or anywhere else in the Bible for that matter. "Ask, and it will be given to you; seek, and you will find; knock, and it will be opened to you."

Aren't you thankful for this? What a wonderful thing to remember on this Day One that in a world full of fine print, God's promises are pure and simple.

Today Is DAY ONE

Anxiety

Do not be anxious about anything, but in every situation, by prayer and petition, with thanksgiving, present your requests to God. And the peace of God, which transcends all understanding, will guard your hearts and your minds in Christ Jesus.

PHILIPPIANS 4:6-7 NIV

One of my friends has a fear of flying. Looking at him you wouldn't guess he would be afraid of much of anything. He's a big guy. He looks like he could have played college football. But at 35,000 feet, he's an absolute wreck. He breaks out in a cold sweat and is startled by even the slightest turbulence. Does he enjoy feeling that anxiety? Of course not.

Do you enjoy having anxious feelings? No, nobody does. Millions of people struggle with anxiety on some level, and taking one look around this world we live in, we shouldn't be surprised. There is much to be anxious about. But to all of us who are anxious, God offers His peace. And not just any peace, but "the peace of God, which transcends all understanding." What a wonderful thought—by bringing our anxiety to God, we can receive a peace that resides high above any turbulence that causes anxiety in our lives. And this transcendent peace will guard our hearts and minds.

What do you tend to feel anxious about? Your health? Your family? Your finances? Your relationship with someone special? Present these anxious feelings to God. Pray for His peace to push away any anxiety today. Then rest in knowing that God will guard your heart and mind in every situation you commit to Him.

A Prayer for My Words Today

May the words of my mouth and the meditation of my heart be pleasing to you, O Lord, my rock and my redeemer.

Psalm 19:14 NLT

You don't need me to tell you how powerful and influential words can be. A positive word of encouragement or kindness can turn a bad day around in an instant. A rude response from a co-worker or harsh statement shouted from a spouse can ruin what might have been a great day. And just as the words of others have the power to swing your day and your mood in one direction or another, your words have the power and influence to do the same to the world around you.

James called the tongue a "flame of fire" (James 3:6 NLT), highlighting the potential our words have to corrupt our whole bodies and the world around us. Proverbs tells us, "Death and life are in the power of the tongue" (18:21), and "Gracious words are like a honeycomb, sweetness to the soul and health to the body" (16:24). Your children need to hear sweet words of encouragement today, not words spoken at the end of a short fuse. The waitress at the diner needs to hear a patient word, not an annoyed and hurried demand of quicker service. Your spouse needs to hear how amazing he or she is, not a list of all the ways he or she doesn't measure up to your standards.

Ask God on this Day One to fill your mouth with gracious words. What a wonderful daily prayer! "May the words of my mouth and the meditation of my heart be pleasing to you, O Lord."

Today Is DAY ONE

Remember the Poor

They asked us to remember the poor, the very thing I was eager to do.

GALATIANS 2:10

In this portion of the letter to the Galatians, the apostle Paul recounts his meeting with church pillars James, Cephas, and John. They accepted Paul's confession of faith, received him as a brother in the Lord, and agreed that he and Barnabas should work among the Gentiles. Then they added that Paul and Barnabas should remember the poor. Paul, of course, was eager to do so.

We too should be eager to remember the poor—not just to pray for them but also to put feet to our prayers by being generous with ministries that help the poor. And we should look for ways to offer hands-on help ourselves.

We must remember that the love of riches is a snare and that "only with difficulty will a rich person enter the kingdom of heaven" (Matthew 19:23). The gospel in action motivates those who have money to help those who do not. The rich man may have advantages over the poor man in this present world, but he has no advantage over the poor man in God's eyes.

When we minister to the poor, we may be ministering to angels unaware...or to the Lord in disguise.

Valuable to God

Fear not, therefore; you are of more value than many sparrows

MATTHEW 10:31

Do you ever feel useless, like, *God, why am I here?* You don't see your purpose, you don't think you're especially good at anything, and people rarely affirm you in any meaningful way. You feel as if you're just taking up space.

I think at some time or another everyone has felt a bit like that. It happens when our self-worth is tied to our fluctuating feelings or when we listen to the lies of the enemy.

God has a different way of determining our value. He put a price on us that set our value for eternity. For good days and for bad, horrific, why-am-I-still-alive days. That price was the death of Jesus.

In short, the most valuable thing in the universe to God—His Son—became the payment for you to live forever. That's the value you hold in God's eyes.

Today is Day One. Live today with the knowledge that your value to God is great indeed. In fact, nothing is more valuable to God than your soul. He proved that by sending His Son to die on a cross for our sins.

Yesterday, Today, Forever

Jesus Christ is the same yesterday and today and forever.
HEBREWS 13:8

Have you noticed that many restaurants and businesses tend to highlight how long they've been around? You might see an old diner that boasts, "Established 1957" on its sign. This is a way of communicating to the customer that the business has a solid history, a good reputation, and a legacy of unchanging quality. I saw a sign on a food truck that said, "Established 2015." That sign didn't quite instill the same confidence.

But even the best products or businesses occasionally fail to live up to their standards of quality. The same can be said for people.

As hard as we may try to live consistently, we are far from perfect. Most days, I feel like a yo-yo—I'm up and down and up and down. When my circumstances change, my moods change. And when my moods change, my attitude changes. And when my attitude changes, the way I treat other people changes. And so on, and so on.

Scripture tells us there is only One who is unchanging. Jesus Christ is the same yesterday and today and forever. When you feel as if everything around you is constantly changing, doesn't it feel good to know that Jesus is completely consistent? He stays the same. The same Counselor. The same Healer. The same Father. The same Friend. Established more than 2000 years ago and guaranteed to stay the same forever, the unchanging One is your solid rock today and every day.

What Is Church, Anyway?

Therefore encourage one another and build one another up, just as you are doing.

1 Thessalonians 5:11

For some people, church can be boring. I don't feel that way. I'm blessed to be part of a good church, and I hope you are too. If you aren't, I hope you can find one. A good church fellowship can sure come in handy during tough times. And when you're not going through tough times yourself, someone else at church is, and you might be the one to help them.

The word *church* literally means "called out ones." When we came to Christ, God called us out of the world system and into His kingdom. So it should seem natural that sometimes we want to be with others who have been "called out" to fellowship and praise our Lord.

If you're discouraged about church, I hope you'll do something about it. You can...

- Stay and help your church be a better church.
- Find a different church where you feel at home.
- Stay home and watch Netflix.

Okay, that last one is a joke...I hope. Really, the first two are your best options. Pray about which to choose. If you're in a good church, thank God for bringing you there by divine appointment. Resolve to be an encouragement to others who need what you have.

Let this be Day One of praying for your church and its leadership.

Today Is DAY ONE

Mission Walks the Halls

> By this everyone will know that you are my disciples, if you love one another.
>
> JOHN 13:35 NIV

I was invited to sing for a corporate event in South Dakota for a special group of people. It was a hospital staff who had adopted a special theme for the year—"Mission walks the halls." I asked the director of the hospital what exactly that meant. He replied that the doctors and nurses are encouraged to treat their rounds in the hospital less like a job and more like a mission. It's a mission to show love to a hurting world in everything they do.

Many times in our mission as disciples of Christ, we talk the talk. But how often does our mission include walking the halls of our workplaces? How often in our mission do we walk through the airports or city streets or high school cafeterias or college classrooms?

Jesus's plan for your life is that your love for Him will spill over into a love for the world around you; that your relationship with Him wouldn't be just a job you have to do, but a mission you're passionate to accomplish. Ask God to show you how to make this your Day One of a mission that walks the halls.

Guarding My Eyes

I will set no wicked thing before mine eyes.
PSALM 101:3 KJV

Have you noticed how hard it is to keep your eyes from straying these days? You wake up on Day One and claim God's fresh mercies that are new every morning as you head out into your day. Then you see a suggestive advertisement, or you notice someone wearing revealing clothing, or an inappropriate picture pops up on your Instagram account.

Later you catch a little TV, and it's almost impossible to escape the sexual impurity that's so in-your-face in today's world. Your curiosity tempts you to watch the next scene. Before you know it, your eyes have been captured, and your brain and the rest of your body quickly follow.

There's no question that we have more visual temptations than ever before. However, the remedy is still the same. Turn away from images that you know will lead you where you don't want to go. Unsubscribe to TV channels that cause you to stumble. Memorize the verse above and others you can use as quick reminders to look away. Install software programs on your computer to provide accountability when you're on the Internet.

Being a Christian doesn't mean you live in a world free of temptation. Actually, the moment you make the decision to fix your eyes on God, you become an even bigger target for the enemy, who would love nothing more than to see you fall into sin today. As long as you live in this broken world, you will face temptation, and your eyes will be tempted to stray.

So be prepared on this Day One, and know that God promises that when you are tempted, "he will also provide a way out so that you can endure it" (1 Corinthians 10:13 NIV).

Today Is DAY ONE

Along the Way

As [Jesus] was going into a village, ten men
who had leprosy met him...When he saw them,
he said, "Go, show yourselves to the priests."
And as they went, they were cleansed.

LUKE 17:12,14 NIV

At the end of every year, I sit down with my journal and revisit some of my favorite experiences of the past 12 months. It's fun to reminisce and remember some of the amazing people I met and places I saw.

I'm often surprised that the concerts I write about in my journal aren't the ones I would have expected in my list of favorites. I would have thought my top-ten list would include shows with the biggest audiences or most enthusiastic crowds.

I remember events like a Sunday morning inside the walls of a Florida maximum-security prison. There was no fancy light show, and I didn't sell a single CD. But there were plenty of tears streaming down the faces of the inmates as their hands were raised in worship. I remember being tired that day and nearly canceling the prison visit to conserve my energy for the "big" show that night. I remember crying and singing and thanking God for showing me that this prison was where He wanted me to be.

Some of our most meaningful ministry moments happen on the way to where we think we're going. Jesus displayed this truth throughout His ministry. Many of His miracles took place while He was on His way to a destination.

It's okay to set out with a clear destination in mind today. Just ask God to help you not to overlook how He might want to use you along the way.

Playing the Cards You Are Dealt

The LORD blessed the latter days of Job
more than his beginning.

JOB 42:12

Have you ever been dealt into a card game and picked up your cards only to discover they're practically useless? You can't make anything out of this two of hearts, nine of spades, jack of diamonds, and three and six of clubs. What to do? Just fold and wait for the next hand?

Life can be like that. We can be dealt some cards at birth or somewhere along the way that we didn't choose and that will make for a tough life. In such cases, we can't just fold and wait for the next hand. We have to play the cards we were dealt.

Our comfort is that we know the Dealer in this game of life. He knows the cards we hold, and He watches as we play what we've been dealt.

I think about poor Job. He was sure dealt a poor hand. In fact, he lost everything he had in the game. Still, he didn't give up hope. Sure, he was discouraged, but God was watching and had a plan. That plan involved a completely new hand that would put him back on top.

If you're dealt a hand of five cards that add up to nothing, know that God can turn every one of those dud cards into wild cards that add up to a winning hand. Just ask Job.

Starting Small

Do not despise these small beginnings,
for the Lord rejoices to see the work begin.

Zechariah 4:10 NLT

Sometimes God is the God of small beginnings. We want something big and grand, and we want it now. Or maybe next week. Certainly not several years from now, and definitely not after hard work, discouragement, and waiting.

But hard work, discouragement, and waiting are ingredients in almost any successful endeavor. I put in a lot of hard work. Yes, I faced discouragement, and I had to wait. Of the three, I think waiting might have been the hardest. Like most people, I didn't want to begin at the beginning. I was reluctant to pay the price to get where I felt God wanted me. But then, this was my calling, wasn't it? How could I not put in the long hours and hard work, endure the discouragement, and wait for God to produce the fruit in His time, not mine?

I don't know what you're called to do in life, but it's likely to be challenging. You will probably start small—maybe you already have—and you will undoubtedly face discouragement and rejection.

Maybe this is Day One of your breakthrough. Or maybe it will be another day in God's waiting room. Can you be content either way?

Don't despise your small beginnings. Be faithful with whatever God puts in front of you today.

Today Is
DAY ONE

Don't Fake it!

Let love be genuine.

ROMANS 12:9

Make no mistake—Christianity is real, Christ is real, and the Christian life is a real life. It's the only real life as far as I'm concerned. But sometimes instead of committing to the real thing, we can begin to fake it. We can act the way we think Christians are supposed to act, speak the way they're supposed to speak, and smile the way they're supposed to smile.

Growing up in the church, the son of a preacher, I mastered the art of looking the part of a good Christian. But over and over again, God shows me that He hasn't called me to merely look the part. He wants me to live the part. In the Bible, God never asks us to be something we're not. If you're tempted to fake it, don't do it. If Day One isn't going so well, say so. Tell a friend. Tell God. You'll get through it.

When you smile today, make it a real one. When you praise Him, mean it. Because when He tells you He loves you, He's telling the truth—believe it!

Today Is DAY ONE

Loving My Enemies

If possible, so far as it depends on you, live peaceably with all.
ROMANS 12:18

D o you have any enemies? I hope not, but to be honest, most people have at least one or two difficult people in their lives.

What can you do about the difficult people in your life? You've asked them to change. You've prayed for them to change. You may even have nagged them to change. But they won't or can't change. They are who they are.

So what does that mean for you? It means either you need to move on and wish them well without you in their life, or *you* might need to do the changing. For most people, the second option is the most practical but also the hardest.

Here are a couple of keys to making the change a bit easier. First, you're going to have to pray for them. Not for them to change—you've already tried that. Just pray for them. Bless them in prayer. Pray for whatever needs you know they have. Second, you may have to set some boundaries with them. You will need to explain to them that because you are obviously a challenge to them (as they are to you), it would be best for both of you to step back from the relationship. Maybe a regularly scheduled visit or phone call could be set up. Whatever boundaries you feel are necessary will be appropriate.

Today is your Day One of being at peace with all people, so much as is possible and in your power to do. And don't be too proud to admit when the changes must start with you.

Today Is
DAY ONE

Every Thought

Jesus knew what they were thinking, so he asked them, "Why do you have such evil thoughts in your hearts?"
MATTHEW 9:4 NLT

On more than one occasion, Jesus responded to someone's thoughts. He knew what people were thinking and addressed the issue even before they spoke. Of all the miracles Jesus performed, this ability to read people's thoughts tends to fly under our radar. But don't miss the miracle here. Jesus was doing something incredible, and He's teaching us something incredible all these years later. He was and is all-knowing.

He knew the thoughts of the Pharisees, the disciples, and even the strangers who crossed His path. And He knows your thoughts too. Today, people pay good money searching for someone who can tell them something about themselves. People have their palms read, they visit psychics, they go to people who study facial expressions...all to learn more about themselves. But Jesus is the only one who knows every single thought you have. And just as He answered people's thoughts in Scripture, He will answer your thoughts even before you speak to Him. This knowledge can be an absolute game changer in your prayer life. He is present in your thought process, and He knows what's going on in your heart and mind at all times. So you can pray continually and hear from God continually without even saying a word.

Lay your thoughts, as well as your words, before Him today.

The List

[Love] keeps no record of wrongs.
1 CORINTHIANS 13:5 NIV

I like to work from lists. They help me stay organized. But there's one list I don't make anymore. That's a list of all my wrongs, shortcomings, sins, and failures.

Have you made a list like this? Go ahead and write it all down. Every sin you can think of, every failure, every stupid thing you regret doing, all the words you said you wish you could take back. Get real with this list. Don't hold back.

After you've made the list, hold it up to the Lord as an offering. Then tear it into a million little pieces and toss those pieces in the trash. Better yet, burn them. Make them go away forever. After all, that's what God has done.

This list you just tore up was simply a visual representation of how you should look at all your junk in the past. It's gone. Don't hang onto it. Let it go!

Day One is always better when we fully let go of the past.

Today Is **DAY ONE**

Same Day, Different Seashells

All Scripture is inspired by God and is useful to teach us what is true and to make us realize what is wrong in our lives. It corrects us when we are wrong and teaches us to do what is right.

2 TIMOTHY 3:16 NLT

One of my favorite things about family vacations is taking early morning walks on the beach with my oldest daughter. She's the early riser in our family. Most people use vacations to catch up on rest, but my daughter makes sure that doesn't apply to me.

She's my six a.m. wake-up call. So after a stop at the local coffee shop, we ride our bikes down to the beach in search of seashells. On a recent walk, we turned back to go over the same stretch of sand we had just combed through, and to my surprise, I noticed there were new seashells waiting to be discovered. We had just covered that ground moments ago, but there they were, delivered by the tide—a whole new batch of shells for us to choose from.

God's Word is like that stretch of beach. Just when you think you've uncovered all that Scripture has to teach you, you'll be amazed by something new that God reveals to you as you commit to faithfully read His Word. Maybe you don't feel like it today. Maybe you're struggling to find the motivation to open your Bible. Maybe it just feels like something you've read a thousand times. If so, ask God to help you see Scripture with new eyes. God's Word is alive, and every day you can come to His Word with great anticipation. When you do, He will show you something new about His love, His power, and His plan for your life.

Live Up, Part 1

Whoever claims to live in him must live as Jesus did.
1 JOHN 2:6 NIV

When I first moved to Nashville to pursue a career as a songwriter, I was given some great advice from a trusted source who was already where I hoped to be someday: "Write up." He was saying that I should seek out the songwriters I most admired, writers who were more experienced than me, and get in a room with them as often as possible to write songs. He wasn't encouraging me simply to rub shoulders with big-time writers. He wasn't giving me advice about seeking status. Rather, he was encouraging me to gain wisdom. The more time I spent around those great songwriters, learning from them and watching their process, the more I would become like them with sharpened skills in the craft of songwriting.

The same is true in our efforts to become more like Christ. After all, that's our true goal in this life. God loves us just the way we are, but from that starting point, He's leading us to be more like Him in every way. Just as I was encouraged to "write up," we are all encouraged to *live* up.

How do we do this? God doesn't expect us to figure out how to be more Christlike on our own. If we want to become more like Christ, we must spend more time with Christ. Time in God's presence, praying and consuming Scripture, is essential in learning what it means to be more like Jesus.

Live Up, Part 2

Grow in the grace and knowledge of our
Lord and Savior Jesus Christ. To him be the
glory both now and forever! Amen.
2 Peter 3:18 NIV

Scripture tells us that becoming more like Christ isn't an instant change, but a process. "Grow in the grace..." A seed doesn't instantly sprout into a plant from the first drop of water. It takes time and constant nourishment.

Yesterday I shared with you about "living up." The first way to grow into the image of Christ is to spend time with Him. Another essential key to spiritual growth is seeking out relationships with people whose character and spiritual walk you admire. Just as I try to surround myself with songwriters whom I admire in the hopes of becoming a better songwriter myself, this same principle applies in our spiritual lives.

Perhaps there's someone at your church that you admire, someone more mature and experienced. In Scripture, Timothy had Paul. The disciples had Jesus. Whom do you have?

Seeking out accountability and wisdom from others isn't always easy, especially for guys. We tend to isolate ourselves and internalize our spiritual walk. But we need each other. Scripture calls us to "spur one another on toward love and good deeds" (Hebrews 10:24 NIV).

Don't isolate yourself and expect to grow spiritually. Ask yourself, *Whom do I have?* If you can't answer that question, ask God to show you who that someone should be. "Live up" in your life by looking to others who can spur you on and help you grow.

Mended

My beloved is mine, and I am his.
SONG OF SOLOMON 2:16

When you look in the mirror, what do you see? Just a reflection of your face? On this Day One, as you look into the mirror, I hope you to see a miracle looking back at you.

You *are* a miracle. From the tips of your toes to the top of your head, you are one splendid miracle. You may see yourself as ugly or unattractive. God sees you as beautiful. You may see whatever labels others have put on you. God sees the label He put on you—*beloved.*

You see your brokenness, but God sees how He's mended you and is still mending you. Your life is far from over. God is at work in you every single Day One—especially this Day One.

Maybe you've had a rougher life than others. Maybe rougher than what you expected. So now you see "damaged goods" in the mirror. You see your wounds. But God sees fading scars that barely reveal past hurts. Scars that will be even fainter tomorrow.

Where we tend to see an end, God sees a beginning. Every day is Day One. A fresh beginning and a day when the scars are fainter than yesterday. So hold on, it's not the end. You see wounded, God sees mended.

Anything Is Possible

With God all things are possible.
MATTHEW 19:26

Have you ever felt as if you were at the end of your rope? Sure you have. We all have. But for the most part, we're at the end of different ropes. A health crisis, a lost job, a broken relationship, a prison sentence...these are just a few ropes we can find ourselves at the end of.

The great news is that Day One brings a new length of rope and a new hope for all of us regardless of our situation. That new length of rope is where grace is. Reach out your hand to find that next stretch of rope. Take hold. Hang on.

Remember that God's rope has no end. He offers more rope every Day One. Remember too that He is the God of the impossible. In fact, God laughs at the word *impossible*.

With a God like that, a God who can turn messes into miracles, anything is possible.

Born for This

He who had set me apart before I was born...called me by his grace.

GALATIANS 1:15

What exactly were you born for? Do you know?

I think life is mostly about finding and living out God's purpose for us. Along the way, we make a few detours.

Okay, so that's obviously not my mission in life.

Whoops, wrong turn there!

But this road looked so promising!

Finally, we find it. *Ah! So this is why I'm here! Thank You, Lord!* Such a fine thing when we find out why we were born...how we're here to do a specific work that helps other people in some way.

We often spend Day One finding that right avenue to our purpose. Then one day or one week or one month, we discover we're actually on the right road and probably have been for some time but just didn't realize it.

Know this today—you were born to live out God's plan for this Day One as it brings you closer to everything He has for you.

Heaven Is the Hope

Let not your hearts be troubled. Believe in God; believe also in me. In my Father's house are many rooms. If it were not so, would I have told you that I go to prepare a place for you? And if I go and prepare a place for you, I will come again and will take you to myself, that where I am you may be also.

JOHN 14:1-3

We can't let ourselves get too comfortable here on earth. God has a better home waiting for us. That home is real—more real than this earth—and it's in heaven.

Living in this temporary home can be tough. It's like we're grounded here until God gives us the nod to come to our heavenly home.

Meanwhile, every Day One we sense an aching...a longing to be with God forever. God says to us, "I'll bring you home after the story of your earthly life has been told in full."

He gives us grace for the pain in this life. He gives us peace in the chaos and uncertainty of earth. He gives us a promise to build our life on. A promise that will be fulfilled in His own good time.

Walk through this Day One as though you're just passing through this life—because that's the truth. You won't be here much longer. Stay your course. Let God tell your story. And let the hope of heaven and an eternity in the presence of Jesus be your motivation to finish strong.

O Me of Little Faith

I believe; help my unbelief!
MARK 9:24

I have not found a verse in the Bible that more honestly sums up the human struggle between faith and doubt than these words. They were spoken by a man whose son was possessed by an evil spirit. "I believe; help my unbelief!"

The father had just told Jesus that his son had been possessed since he was a little boy. One can imagine that after days had turned into months and years with no change in his son's condition, doubt had set in. Yet something made him reach out to the Messiah. He had heard of this man. Word of His many miracles had spread. Driven by a father's love and what little bit of faith he could muster, he brought his son to Jesus. Come to think of it, this man was actually asking Jesus for two miracles that day—healing for his son and the restoration of his own faith.

Jesus answered both requests.

During difficult seasons of life, many of my prayers echo this same sentiment. *Lord, I believe. I mean, I want to believe. I would like to think I believe. God, I'm struggling to believe. Oh, help that part of me that doesn't believe You are in control.* Be honest when you talk to God. He can handle your doubt. He can handle your fear. Come to Him with the same request the father made. Ask Him to help your unbelief today, and rest in knowing that all He asks of you is to have enough faith to look to Him.

He'll do the rest.

Abiding in the Vine

Abide in me, and I in you. As the branch cannot bear fruit by itself, unless it abides in the vine, neither can you, unless you abide in me.

JOHN 15:4

Just when I think I can do something well—like love others, or be a servant to others, or live out the fruit of the Spirit—God shows me how far I am from His goal for me. He doesn't leave me there though. God is an encourager, so when He shows me my lack, He also shows me His supply.

His supply is like that of a vine to the branches. The branches can't do anything on their own. Separated from the vine, the branches are nothing but firewood. But if the branches are connected to the vine, the vine can supply them with life.

Jesus is the vine, and we are the branches. Without Him, we can do nothing, regardless of how hard we try in our own strength. On this Day One, stop and consider whether you're trying to produce fruit on your own. If you are, is it working? Wouldn't it be better to abide in Jesus, the vine, and let His life flow through you?

Speaking Your Faith

Behold, I am sending you out as sheep in the midst of wolves, so be wise as serpents and innocent as doves.
MATTHEW 10:16

So, what do you think about _____?" the person across the table asks you. They know you're a Christian, and they're putting you on the spot by asking you about a hot-button topic to see what your reaction is. You can guess the topics. There are plenty to choose from these days.

How do you answer? You don't want to sound judgmental or critical, but you want to be faithful to God's truth. In times like these, we have to be wise as serpents but gentle as doves. It would be wrong just to spout off mindless Christian clichés. Besides, most important topics can't be properly addressed in sound bites.

It will help to have thought ahead about what you really believe about social issues based on God's Word. Just remember, sometimes God's answers aren't palatable to unbelievers, but they are always wise, just, and full of grace. And that's how our answers should be too. Most importanly, ask God to give you the right words to speak whenever you're given a chance to express your faith. He put you in the situation for a reason. Keep your eyes on Him and listen for His leading.

In Light of Eternity

Your steadfast love is before my eyes,
and I walk in your faithfulness.
PSALM 26:3

Every Day One is part of our unique pathway to the future. Each of our decisions has a ripple effect on the days ahead. How then can we decide correctly?

One way is to think in the light of eternity. Start with this: *Will this decision have eternal ramifications?* In most cases, the answer will be no. But when the answer is yes, that's time to pray, weigh the options carefully in the light of eternity, and perhaps seek advice from those you trust.

When the decision to be made seems like a small one, don't be too quick to dismiss it with a flip of the coin. Surprisingly, small decisions often end up having the most impact on us. This is where walking in faith daily comes in handy. Decisions made in faith, after prayer and deliberation, are usually the right ones. And if you're truly walking in faith, God will use even the wrong decisions for your good. Faith is the key.

When faced with decisions today, ask God to help you be mindful of the eternal value of the choices you make, not just the here and now. When we hold our lives up to the light of eternity, everything looks clearer.

Prayer Breaks

The LORD has heard my plea;
the LORD accepts my prayer.

PSALM 6:9

I'm a big believer in prayer, and not just when I have a need or am in trouble. I believe in prayer the way I believe in breakfast, lunch, and dinner. Prayer is spiritual food I need daily.

Eating a meal takes about 20 or 30 minutes. I don't usually pray that long all at one time. (Well, on some days I do, but not every day.) But I do sprinkle some prayer breaks throughout each day. I don't mean I find a secret place, get down on my knees, fold my hands, look up to heaven, and pray. No, I just pause a few times a day when I can, consider God's goodness to me, lift up some thoughts or words of praise, and then go back to what I was doing.

I'm not suggesting these prayer breaks take the place of a daily quiet time, when we take time to pray at length. But I see them as important supplements to a regular prayer time.

On this Day One, keep your eyes open for opportunities to turn your thoughts toward heaven and offer up thanksgiving, praise, and requests before God.

These prayer breaks are like short meals or healthy snacks. They're also like vitamins. They can help us grow spiritually strong as we pause every now and then to reaffirm our dependence on God.

Today Is

DAY ONE

This Is the Way, Walk in It

Your ears shall hear a word behind you, saying,
"This is the way, walk in it," when you turn to
the right or when you turn to the left.

ISAIAH 30:21

Have you ever been lost in the forest? Or in a building where you didn't know the way out? It's not a good feeling, is it? You might even panic and run in any direction, right or wrong, just to keep moving. Or you might stop and sit down until someone comes and finds you.

Life can be that way. We can go along with no real direction and suddenly realize we don't know where we are. What do we do then?

Pray first. Then just get up and do the next thing you know to do. It might be like taking one small step in an unknown direction. Listen for God's voice to direct you. His voice can come through the Bible, the counsel of friends and family, circumstances, or a distinct impression in prayer.

The thing to remember is that although God says, "This is the way, walk in it" to all of us who ask Him, the specific direction will usually be different for each of us. My path is not your path, nor is yours mine. We get lost when we try to walk on someone else's path. Stay true to your unique journey with God. Trust Him and move ahead one Day One at a time.

My Best Days Are Ahead of Me

If God is for us, who can be against us?

ROMANS 8:31

When you consider every fresh day as Day One, you can look forward with confidence not only to *this* Day One but also to every Day One to come. Truly, your best days are ahead of you, not behind you. That attitude keeps us focused on trusting God to use us in the days ahead. Where will you be a year from now? Five years from now? Twenty years?

God knows the answer. All I know for sure is that God is for us, not against us. He has planned to work everything for our good. That means that what appear to be setbacks are really God's strategies to move us where we weren't expecting to go. Trust Him to keep you in just the right place at just the right time—regardless of how many years are ahead.

Believing God for your best days to come is an exercise in faith that produces awesome results. Go forward in confidence today, knowing that your best days will always be ahead of you, all the way until the day you leave this earth and enter eternity.

Today Is DAY ONE

I Don't Have to Stay Here

He will command his angels concerning you
to guard you in all your ways.
On their hands they will bear you up,
lest you strike your foot against a stone.

Psalm 91:11-12

Why do we stay in ruts or habits or lifestyles that we hate or that are bad for us?

Sometimes we're afraid to try something new. We feel safe in familiar circumstances, even if they're not good. We're often reluctant to break free, make changes, and start on a journey to a happier life.

You don't have to be afraid of an unknown pathway when you serve a known God. We should be careful when moving out of a bad situation, but we shouldn't stay where we are when we're afraid or in danger of harm. And even if we're just stuck...that can be discouraging.

Today is Day One—your opportunity to make a great, new start. Can you envision a way to move on from where you are now? Life is change. Slow change, fast change. Either one in God's hands is good change. What have you got to lose? Don't waste another day stuck in a place where you know you shouldn't be. Ask God for the strength to step out in faith and let Him lead you forward.

The Clock Is Tickin'

I trust in you, O LORD;
I say, "You are my God."
My times are in your hand.

PSALM 31:14-15

Sometimes I wish Day One had 28 hours. So many things I want to do! How about you? Could you use more hours in your Day One? Yeah, I thought so.

Thinking of that makes me realize how precious time is. No matter how hard we wish, pray, or tinker with our clocks, we all have only 24 hours in a day. Ask a dying man, and he'll tell you each hour is precious and shouldn't be wasted.

It shouldn't take a serious diagnosis for us to appreciate that every day is worth its weight in gold. And just as we wouldn't waste gold, we should never waste time. Sure, we should allow time for rest and recreation. Even Jesus did that. That's not wasting time. But I can think of a few ways I waste time in my life, and I bet you can identify some ways you do in yours. How can you redeem that time—time you can never get back?

On this Day One, watch for ways in which you waste time (remember, don't count recreation or rest) and ask God to help you add time to your days by eliminating the time-wasters from your life.

The Fully Prepared Day

Be strong and courageous...
for it is the LORD your God who goes with you.
He will not leave you or forsake you.

DEUTERONOMY 31:6

The Latin phrase *carpe diem* ("seize the day") helps us see each day as Day One. Every day is ours for the taking. Regardless of what we face, we can do so with courage, hope, and faith that God goes before us in all we do. God has seen our today and our tomorrow, and He knows we can handle whatever comes our way. There are no surprises to God.

God has, in fact, prepared the day for us. The question is, are we prepared for the day? We get ready by expecting God to bless us, guide our every step, and work all our setbacks to a good end.

Come to think of it, today isn't yours for the taking. It's yours for the giving. Giving each day back to the One who gives you life is the best way to walk forward fully prepared for what lies ahead.

Pondering Eternity

Grow in the grace and knowledge of our Lord and Savior Jesus Christ. To him be the glory both now and to the day of eternity. Amen.

2 Peter 3:18

Do you ever think about eternity? I sure do. Can you imagine what it will be like to live forever in a sinless environment with God our Father wiping away every single tear?

As we wait for eternity, we can have joy in this life because for us who believe in Christ, eternity begins now. By living for Christ while on earth, we experience a taste of what heaven will be like. Every so often something happens that gives me a glimpse of eternity. Sometimes it happens when I'm writing songs or singing. In a way, music becomes a language in which God and I communicate. Other glimpses come in the surge of love I feel when looking at my wife and daughters.

This is Day One of your forever life. Eternity begins now. Let every glimpse of something beautiful that you witness today remind you of the beauty that awaits on the other side. And let that beauty make you heart long for heaven and more with each passing day.

I Can't Stop Looking Back

Cast your burden on the LORD,
and he will sustain you.

PSALM 55:22

Sometimes things happen we can't seem to get past. An event or situation haunts us, and we can't fully embrace Day One as a new beginning. When that happens, we need to break the power of that crippling memory. We need to stop looking back so we can focus on what's ahead for us. Easier said than done, I know.

One important key is to fully surrender that memory to the Lord...and then leave it with Him. You can do this. Others have done it. So have I.

Whatever happened in the past is redeemable. But redemption comes only through surrender. The next time that memory tries to find its way into your day, refuse to accept it. After all, if you've truly surrendered it to God, it's no longer yours to deal with. Let it go. Cast your past, your painful memories, your hurt, your burdens on the Lord.

Love and Trust

The person who truly loves God is the one who is open to God's knowledge.

1 CORINTHIANS 8:3 TLB

The two go hand in hand. Love and trust. According to Scripture, one is evidence of the other. If we confess with our mouths that we love God but live our lives disregarding the knowledge, instruction, and leading He offers us, how deep does our love for Him really go? Perhaps you've had a relationship with someone that was hindered by your inability to trust them. I know I have. Something was done or said that cut the ties of trust that had been built. Oh, I still had love for that person, but our friendship suffered because that trust bond was broken.

In your relationship with God, you will never have to worry about Him betraying your trust. He is ever faithful, and His knowledge far surpasses the knowledge of even the smartest, most intellectual human beings walking this earth.

Spend a few moments today assessing how you've gone about making decisions in your life lately. Have you displayed trust in God by seeking His knowledge? Or have you been closed off to His offer of knowledge in how to navigate your day?

Often, our lack of trust in God isn't a deliberate act but more of a knee-jerk reaction to circumstances that arise and our natural desire to fix things.

Say this prayer with me: *Lord, I do love You, and I want to trust You every step of the way today. Help my heart and my head to stay open to the knowledge You offer, knowing that Your knowledge will never steer me in the wrong direction. Amen.*

Here Comes the Sun

As your days, so shall your strength be.
DEUTERONOMY 33:25

Day One may bring you some surprises, but you can count on at least one thing—the sun will rise once again. The sun is like a messenger that says, "Here comes a brand-spankin'-new Day One."

The problem is, if clouds hide the sunrise, we don't appreciate it as much as if the weather is fair and the sun shines through.

In order to enjoy each day as Day One, appreciating each new start, we have to get past the need to see the sun shining on our path. All we need to know is that it's there regardless of whether we see it.

Look outside. What's it like? Can you see the sun, or is it rainy and dark? Does it really matter? If you were on an airplane, you'd probably be above the clouds and storm right now. You'd look down and see the dark clouds. Then you'd look out over the blue sky beside you and see that the sun is just as bright as ever.

Don't ever let the clouds tell you there is no sun. You know better. Before long the clouds will move on, and you'll see the sun again. God's promise for you today is that clouds or no clouds, He will give you the strength you need.

My Someday Soon Is Here and Now

Let your eyes look directly forward,
and your gaze be straight before you.

PROVERBS 4:25

When we're young, we envision an awesome future. Someday we'll do this, we'll do that. Someday we'll travel here, we'll travel there. And if you're like me, you might have imagined those things would just happen through the natural course of events...someday.

But they don't. They usually happen after many, many Day Ones of not just imagining the future but also pursuing it. We have to get up and go after what God has for us. It won't just fall into our lap.

What do you want most in life? What does God want most for your life? If the answer to those questions is the same, you're on the right track. But even being on the right track isn't enough. The train has to be chugging down the rails toward the destination.

Today is Day One. It's the day God has called you to chug ahead on the journey to His destination for you. Slowly but surely, move ahead today. Praise God that He's in charge of your trip.

Your someday soon is here and now. Pursue God with all of your heart today, and He will lead you to the life He has planned for you.

So Loved

God so loved the world, that he gave his only Son, that whoever believes in him should not perish but have eternal life.

JOHN 3:16

You've seen signs in ballparks and stadiums that say "John 3:16." Usually they don't even write out the verse because by now just about everyone knows the words. It's probably the most well-known Bible verse of all.

My fear is that the words become so commonplace, we tend to forget the power of the message of God's love for us. For God *so loved* the world...

If there's a verse packed with more emotion than John 3:16, I'd like to know what it is.

John 3:16 is the address of my hope. It contains the words that set me free. They are the reason I can look forward to each day. Every morning is Day One if I can just rehearse again the power of those words—God so loved Matthew West that He gave his only begotten Son, that Matthew should not perish but have eternal life.

John 3:16 will jump-start your dead-battery day. John 3:16 makes your Day One possible. Insert your name into that Scripture like I just did and let your heart be flooded by the reminder that you are so deeply loved by your Savior.

Today Is DAY ONE

Prodigal Parade

When he came to himself, he said, "How many of my father's hired servants have more than enough bread, but I perish here with hunger! I will arise and go to my father."

LUKE 15:17-18

Aren't you glad Jesus came for the prodigals, not those who consider themselves righteous?

I'm a prodigal. My past isn't squeaky clean. I needed someone to save me from myself—and thank God, He did just that.

He does that for all us prodigals who have discovered we were on the wrong road and turned back before it was too late. Turned back to return to our Father. Turned back to living in a way that brings peace of mind, not guilt, shame, or tormenting thoughts.

We turned back to love. We turned back to home. We turned back so this can be Day One of a life of joy, not doubt and gloom.

Sometimes I feel like the poster boy for prodigals. The guy most qualified to lead the prodigal parade. If you're a prodigal, fall in behind me and join our parade. You'll have a lot of company.

All of us have fallen away from what is good and right and true. And just as the father of the prodigal son threw a party upon his son's return, the prodigal parade is a celebration. No matter how far we fall, we are being welcomed back home.

Let the parade begin!

Today Is

DAY ONE

Bread and Water

I am the living bread that came down from heaven. Whoever eats this bread will live forever.

JOHN 6:51 NIV

Several verses in the book of John describe Jesus as bread and water. We know that bread and water are basics our physical bodies need to survive. They are our sustenance. Bread and water equal survival. If you were stranded and starving in the middle of a desert and someone came along and offered you bread and water, you wouldn't respond by saying, "No, thanks. I'm in the mood for a steak and fine wine." When it's a matter of life and death, bread and water are all you need and all you desire.

Jesus is teaching us that what bread and water provide for our bodies, He provides for our souls. Jesus said, "I am the living bread that came down from heaven. Whoever eats this bread will live forever." Jesus is the bread we need for spiritual survival, and this Scripture tells us that it truly is a matter of life and death. Choosing Jesus as your bread and water is the only way to extend your life beyond this momentary life. "Whoever eats this bread will live forever."

We Are the Broken

I have been forgotten like one who is dead;
I have become like a broken vessel.

PSALM 31:12

I don't know how it is that you're broken. I don't know what broke you or how long ago it was or how your healing is coming along. All I know is that because you're a human being, you have experienced some degree of brokenness.

I'm broken too. But long ago I realized that staying broken means staying in pain. It means trying to hide my brokenness, cover my scars, and replay my worst memories.

Then God came along, and healing began.

Being broken is okay, but God allows brokenness only so He can work with us.

Ask yourself, if you were whole in every part of your life, if you were not broken, would you need the Lord as desperately as you do now?

Our needs cry out to God for fulfillment. No needs, no crying out.

This is Day One, so thank God for revealing Himself to you in your brokenness. Remember that the cracks in your life allow the sun to shine through into the darkness. And take comfort in knowing that God takes broken people and turns them into something beautiful. He will do that with your life.

Wonderfully Made

I praise you, for I am fearfully and wonderfully made.
Wonderful are your works;
my soul knows it very well.

PSALM 139:14

The human body is truly amazing! Sometimes I wake up in the morning, wiggle my toes, and thank God for my movable body. (Not that it's actually ready to move out of bed right away!) Sometimes I'm truly aware of how wonderfully made I am, but sometimes I take my body for granted. Probably like you, I often go about my day without really considering how awesome the human body is.

I'm trying to make awareness of my body and gratitude for it a regular part of Day One. I'm also trying to do right by it by eating well and getting exercise and rest. We undermine the potential of Day One when we treat our body with disrespect or aren't thankful for the body we have.

Now wiggle your toes and give thanks!

Jesus in Other People

As each has received a gift, use it to serve one another, as good stewards of God's varied grace.

1 PETER 4:10

Wouldn't it be great to actually see Jesus in person? We'd be flat on our faces in adoration in no time at all. Well, we won't see Jesus this side of heaven. That is, unless...

Unless we see Him in each other—fellow members of His body.

Unless we see Him in those who suffer—"the least of these my brothers."

Unless we see Him in ourselves—His hands and feet in the world.

We're saved by faith, not by our works, but good works are the result, or fruit, of being a Christian. Serving others is how we serve Jesus. And we serve others by doing what Jesus would do for them. I like to think that when we pray for Jesus to flow through us on this Day One, God will set up divine appointments and allow us that privilege. I've seen it happen in my own life.

I'm humbled when God sends someone to represent Jesus to me. They may not even know my need, but someone will come up with the right words or even just a smile or hug, and I feel as if I've been with Jesus.

Go ahead. Give it a try. Be on the lookout for Jesus in other people today. But more importantly, pray and ask for the grace of your Savior to be so radiant that people see Jesus in you.

Today Is DAY ONE

The World Hates

Do not be surprised, brothers, that the world hates you.
1 JOHN 3:13

What? Hated? *Me?*

The people you know well probably don't hate you, but large segments of the general population oppose Christians. Many unbelievers scoff at what we believe, they consider the Bible to be a fairy tale, and they are convinced that there is no afterlife (especially hell!).

So what are we to do about this animosity? I can think of two good biblical responses. The first is to pray for those who hate you (and mean it). This was Jesus's admonition to us: "You have heard that it was said, 'You shall love your neighbor and hate your enemy.' But I say to you, Love your enemies and pray for those who persecute you" (Matthew 5:43-44).

When Stephen, the first Christian martyr, was being stoned, he prayed for the people hurling the rocks. Guess who one of those men was? The apostle Paul, known then as Saul, the Pharisee who hated and persecuted the early Christians (Acts 7:54-60; 8:1-3).

The second response also comes from Jesus: "Blessed are those who are persecuted for righteousness' sake, for theirs is the kingdom of heaven" (Matthew 5:10).

Here Jesus tells us we are blessed when we're persecuted for being a Christian. Ours is the kingdom of heaven. What a blessing! We should gladly suffer verbal abuse (and worse) to be a disciple of Jesus.

As the days grow darker, don't be surprised if the world opposes you. Accept it and be blessed by it.

Random Acts

As God's chosen people, holy and dearly loved,
clothe yourselves with compassion, kindness,
humility, gentleness and patience.

COLOSSIANS 3:12 NIV

I used to see bumper stickers that said "Practice Random Acts of Kindness," and I've always thought every Christian should stick one of those on the back of his or her car.

Some days it seems as if simple kindness is in short supply. More and more people seem to demonstrate a "me first" attitude. For all the evangelism we Christians do with our mouths (which is important!), I wonder if we might be even more effective if we demonstrated the gospel by practicing acts of kindness to other people, including people we don't know.

The funny thing is, I can't give you a suggested list of random acts of kindness. That's because they're indeed random. They're unpredictable. The opportunities are unplanned, and because of that, we must watch for them.

Today, will you agree with me to watch for at least one random act of kindness you can do for someone else? It will make Day One better for you, and it will bless the person on the receiving end.

Brought to Fullness

In Christ all the fullness of the Deity lives in bodily form, and in Christ you have been brought to fullness.

COLOSSIANS 2:9-10 NIV

One of the most amazing things about being a Christian is that in Christ, we have been "brought to fullness." Wow. I don't know about you, but without Christ, I was full of a lot of cruddy stuff—mostly full of Matthew West. Now, I still have to live with Matthew, but he's not in charge anymore. Now I'm full of Christ, and He calls the shots.

Okay, so sometimes I still call the shots, but then, like you, I'm a work in progress. I'm still a growing Christian and will be until the day God takes me home to heaven.

Whom are you full of today? Have you been "brought to fullness" in Christ?

Let this Day One be a day when Christ is seen more fully in you. Step aside and let Him lead the way.

First

Seek first the kingdom of God and his righteousness, and all these things will be added to you.

MATTHEW 6:33

I've found that anytime, at any place, and on any day, my list of priorities are susceptible to falling out of order. I can spend a rich time in God's presence during a morning quiet time and feel His hand gently putting my list of priorities back in order, only to step out the door and find so many things fighting for that number one position on the list. Job, finances, family, friends, substances, status, hobbies…these are just some of the things that can vie for that top spot on someone's list of what matters most.

I was raised by parents who taught me that above all else, God should come first, followed by family, friends, and so on. As I've gotten older, I've learned that my parents were right, but I want to take it even a step further. For our lives to find true fulfillment, God isn't just the number one priority; He is high above any other items on our list. Everything else is a distant second.

You may think, *That sounds harsh! Don't you love your family?* Of course I do. But the Bible makes it clear to us that loving God and seeking His kingdom are our most essential priorities. And when our priorities are in the right order, that's when we're able to have the healthiest relationships with the other people and things on our list. The command to seek first the kingdom of God includes a powerful promise: "And all these things will be added to you."

Throughout this Day One, when you feel your list of priorities slipping out of order, whisper this word—"first"—and remember what really is your first priority. Let all else be added.

Today Is DAY ONE

Love

Love never ends.

1 Corinthians 13:8

The Bible mentions very few things that never end. But love made that short list.

Love never ends.

Another thing that never ends is life—if we know Christ. That's why Scripture says that if we know Christ, we have eternal life. Life that never ends.

I wonder if there's a relationship between these two unending things—love and life.

We read also in the New Testament that "God is love" (1 John 4:8). We know, too, that our eternal life is really life that is in the presence of God. When we receive Christ into our lives, He dwells in our hearts by faith through the Holy Spirit—and so love lives inside us. And that love is eternal.

Today, take some time to ponder that reality. God, who is love, lives in you, and that love will never end. Then tie that thought to the fact that *you* are also eternal. You, the God who is love, and love itself...all without an end.

That truth can change our lives forever!

Today Is DAY ONE

Wisdom

Blessed is the one who finds wisdom,
and the one who gets understanding.

PROVERBS 3:13

Who wants a blessing from God? We all do, right? Well, the book of Proverbs is chock-full of admonitions to be blessed by pursuing wisdom.

That sounds like a no-brainer, but a lot of people don't pursue wisdom. Instead, they pursue money, vocational success, fame, knowledge...In fact, some people think knowledge and wisdom are synonymous. But if you look closely at some very smart and knowledgeable people, you'll notice that some of them lack wisdom. And many wise people are not necessarily walking encyclopedias.

So what's the difference between knowledge and wisdom? I think part of it is that wise people know how to use their knowledge in appropriate ways. Wise people are discerning people. They know by experience and by the Word of God how to act in various situations.

Another aspect of wisdom (also found in the book of Proverbs) is that it begins with the fear of God. Proverbs 9:10 tells us, "The fear of the LORD is the beginning of wisdom."

People don't often preach about fearing God these days, yet the Bible calls it the beginning of wisdom. How can we *not* desire to fear God and become wise?

Here's an assignment. Ask God to help you fear Him in the way that will open the door for more wisdom. This is the key to a blessed life.

Making Melody to the Lord

Be filled with the Spirit, addressing one another in psalms and hymns and spiritual songs, singing and making melody to the Lord with your heart.

EPHESIANS 5:18-19

As a songwriter and musician, I naturally think in terms of melodies and spiritual songs. But in these verses, Paul was addressing all the believers in Ephesus, not just the musicians.

Through Paul, God is urging us to be filled with His Spirit and to sing to one another in hymns and spiritual songs (that's usually part of what happens every Sunday morning) and to make melody to the Lord with our hearts.

To me, making melody in our hearts doesn't necessarily mean singing out loud. In fact, we can make melody with our hearts just about anywhere while we're doing just about anything.

Singing to the Lord with our hearts can dispel depression, give us a new outlook on our problems, and generally de-stress us. Personally, I think every single Day One should find us making melody to the Lord with our hearts at some point during the day—perhaps even often throughout the day.

Today sing to the Lord with your heart. Use an old tune you already know. Or make up a tune by just singing what you feel. God is your audience, and He will love whatever tune you come up with.

Persistent Sin or Persistent Victory?

Sin will have no dominion over you,
since you are not under law but under grace.

ROMANS 6:14

Can I ask you an honest question? Do you still have a problem with a persistent sin—or sins? It's okay to admit it. That's the first step in dealing with it.

God understands your struggle. You probably know the word *gospel* literally means "good news." But good news about what?

Well, good news about two things. One, the good news that *all* your sins are forgiven. You don't have to try to atone for your sins. Jesus did that for you. Second, the source of your sin problem has been dealt with at the cross. That's *very* good news for those of us who have struggled with sin.

Paul tells us the Law came to show us our sin—and that we couldn't keep it. But the Law can't deal with sin—only grace can do that. In the book of Titus, we see a key truth as to how grace helps us deal with persistent sin: "The grace of God has appeared, bringing salvation for all people, training us to renounce ungodliness and worldly passions, and to live self-controlled, upright, and godly lives in the present age" (Titus 2:11-12).

Grace trains us to "renounce ungodliness and worldly passions." Wow. And all this time many of us thought the Law did that! Grace ushers us into a new relationship with God. We overcome persistent sin through a love relationship and through faith in His Word.

Today, I'm praying for you and your battle with persistent sin. I'm praying for you to see yourself as a recipient of God's amazing grace.

Hungry World

Jesus said to them, "I am the bread of life; whoever comes to me shall not hunger, and whoever believes in me shall never thirst."

JOHN 6:35

We live in a hungry world. Thirsty too. And as people eat the dust of this world and drink its acrid waters, they become increasingly dissatisfied. That's where we come in. We were once there ourselves. We ate that dust, drank that water...and then we met a Man who offered us true bread and quenching waters.

We began to sip the water and nibble at the bread and found it was true. Jesus does satisfy. Yes, sometimes we still feel a hunger pang or we thirst, but we now know that those desires serve only to bring us back to Christ. We know by experience that the world's bread and water never satisfy.

Have you thought of evangelism as simply telling others who are hungry and thirsty that we have met a Man who offers the bread of life and living water?

I pray that on this Day One, God will bring someone across your path who needs to hear of this Man, Jesus Christ. I also pray that you will look nowhere else in this world for the nourishment that can be found only in your Savior.

The Reality of Satan

We are not ignorant of [Satan's] designs.
2 Corinthians 2:11

think sometimes we forget we have a powerful enemy. Satan is very smart in coming up with "designs" by which he means to trip us up. He knows which buttons to push to make us doubt God and believe his lies.

However, we must never allow Satan's lies to attach themselves to our hearts and minds. Here's how we deal with Satan's attacks: First, don't be ignorant of his designs. Recognize the triggers he uses to entice us. Lust, anger, jealousy, greed, worldly ambition...he knows which of those sins are our weak points, and he goes after them. Our awareness of his tactics keeps us on guard against his influence.

Second, and even more important, remember that although Satan is a powerful enemy, God is an infinitely more powerful Victor on our behalf. Paul reminds us, "The weapons of our warfare are not of the flesh but have divine power to destroy strongholds. We destroy arguments and every lofty opinion raised against the knowledge of God, and take every thought captive to obey Christ" (2 Corinthians 10:4-5).

Through prayer, we have divine power to destroy Satan's attempts to bring strongholds into our lives. We are victorious as we take every thought captive to Christ.

That is your assignment on this Day One: Do not be ignorant of Satan's designs on you, and respond by praying against his influence and by taking every thought captive to Christ.

Readiness

Watch therefore, for you know neither the day nor the hour.
MATTHEW 25:13

Jesus ended His parable of the ten virgins with these words of caution. The point was that some who wanted to join the bridegroom at the wedding feast were not be able to because they weren't fully prepared when the doors were opened. They had to go buy more oil for their low-burning lamps. The other virgins had made sure they were prepared.

The point for us is that whether we meet Jesus through death or through His return, readiness is the key to entering in. I don't mean to alarm you (unless you're spiritually asleep, in which case, I *do* mean to alarm you), but you may be only weeks, days, or even hours from meeting the Lord through death. We are not guaranteed tomorrow. Today is the day of salvation. Are you ready?

Every single Day One is the day the bridegroom may arrive for you or me. For that reason, on every single Day One, we need to be prepared to meet Him.

Does your lamp have enough oil?

Today Is DAY ONE

The Cry of the Desperate

Hear my prayer, O Lᴏʀᴅ;
let my cry come to you!
Do not hide your face from me
in the day of my distress!
Incline your ear to me;
answer me speedily in the day when I call!

Psᴀʟᴍ 102:1-2

Aren't you glad God is the God of the desperate? The psalmist was clearly in great distress and called out loudly and forcefully to God. This poor guy needs help *now*!

We all have times of desperation. And when you think about it, doesn't desperation have the positive effect of driving us to our knees?

I think God loves the prayers of the desperate for that very reason. The desperate pray-er has realized that only God can help him. Only God can solve a problem like this.

I believe God not only loves and hears our desperate prayers but also answers those pleas. Isn't that what any good father will do when his child is in great distress and calls on him for help?

Are you desperate today? Or is there a problem on the horizon that may result in desperation? If so, I urge you to cry out to God in your distress. Throw a few exclamation points into your prayer, just as the psalmist did.

Let your desperation be your doorway into greater intimacy with your heavenly Father.

Remember Hymns?

When they had sung a hymn, they went out to the Mount of Olives.
MATTHEW 26:30

I write a lot of contemporary songs about the Lord, and I get a lot of positive response from people. But to tell you the truth, I never abandoned the great old hymns of the faith for contemporary music. There's room on my iPod for both!

I like the deep message many old hymns carry. On the opposite page is the text of "How Firm a Foundation," a hymn from the eighteenth century that is still relevant today. I can only pray that a song of mine will be remembered more than a century from now. Today, let the words of this hymn be your confession.

How Firm a Foundation

How firm a foundation, ye saints of the Lord,
Is laid for your faith in His excellent Word!
What more can He say than to you He hath said,
To you, who for refuge to Jesus have fled?

"Fear not, I am with thee, O be not dismayed,
For I am thy God and will still give thee aid;
I'll strengthen thee, help thee, and cause thee to stand,
Upheld by My righteous, omnipotent hand.

"When through the deep waters I call thee to go,
The rivers of sorrow shall not overflow;
For I will be with thee, thy troubles to bless,
And sanctify to thee thy deepest distress.

"When through fiery trials thy pathway shall lie,
My grace, all-sufficient, shall be thy supply;
The flame shall not hurt thee; I only design
Thy dross to consume, and thy gold to refine.

"The soul that on Jesus still leans for repose,
I will not, I will not desert to his foes;
That soul, though all hell should endeavor to shake,
I'll never, no, never, no, never forsake."

Memories

This day shall be for you a memorial day, and you shall keep it as a feast to the LORD; throughout your generations, as a statute forever, you shall keep it as a feast.

EXODUS 12:14

The Israelites were to keep the Passover meal as a memorial, as a "statute forever" to remind future generations of God's faithfulness. At other places in the Old Testament, God instructed the Hebrew people to set up memorial stones as a reminder of the victory the Lord granted them at that place.

Most of us don't build memorials to celebrate God's faithfulness, but we do have memories that can serve as memorials of God coming through for us. Surely you have good memories of the day you were born again. Maybe the date God brought your mate to you. Or launched you into ministry. Or maybe the day He spared you from a tragic accident.

Memories of God's faithfulness are important for the same reason God's people in the Old Testament erected memorials or held feasts of remembrance. When times get tough, we can look back and remember how God has brought us through other fiery trials.

What are your best memories of God's faithfulness? Today, recall those memories and savor them for a while. They are fuel for your future faith.

Today Is DAY ONE

A Good Name

A good name is to be chosen rather than great riches.
PROVERBS 22:1

What's the first thing people think of when they hear your name?

I hope when someone mentions Matthew West, they think well of me. But a good name doesn't come naturally. It has to be earned and then maintained. I know good people who made one bad mistake and destroyed their reputation. I think of some famous athletes who were applauded for their achievements one year and booed the next year because of their drug use.

Every Day One is a chance to build a good reputation. Or ruin it. Or begin restoring it.

Here are some ways to build and keep a good name:

- Be honest.
- Watch your tongue (don't gossip, swear, brag, or lie).
- Pay your bills on time.
- Keep your word.
- Help others when you can (even when they need help moving!).

You'll probably have a chance to do one or more of these items today. Don't let the opportunity slip by. A good name is the result of doing the right thing every chance you have.

Your Creative Best

Let every skillful craftsman among you come and make all that the Lord has commanded.
Exodus 35:10

God gave very specific directions for the building of the tabernacle. It required "skilled craftsmen" to make all that the Lord commanded. God, of course, was the one who gave the craftsmen their skills, particularly Bezalel.

Look at this passage later in Exodus 35:

> Then Moses said to the people of Israel, "See, the Lord has called by name Bezalel the son of Uri, son of Hur, of the tribe of Judah; and he has filled him with the Spirit of God, with skill, with intelligence, with knowledge, and with all craftsmanship, to devise artistic designs, to work in gold and silver and bronze, in cutting stones for setting, and in carving wood, for work in every skilled craft (Exodus 35:30-33).

Do you have an artistic ability? Are you skilled with a craft? Can you make music? Write? Knit? Act? Teach? Dance? You must know that God gave you the skills you possess. Even if you also took lessons (as I did with music) and practiced your skill, God birthed those natural abilities within you.

God's people are creative people, reflecting His own creative nature. May your Day One always be filled with the utmost creativity in whatever you do for the Lord.

Today Is DAY ONE

Works of Darkness

Take no part in the unfruitful works of darkness, but instead expose them.

EPHESIANS 5:11

We live in world of spiritual darkness. And it seems to be becoming darker each passing year. So what is our response to the "works of darkness" we see?

First, we are to take no part in them ourselves. We are to stay far away from darkness. We are, after all, children of the light. What then do we have to do with darkness?

Second, we are to expose them. We do this because darkness is dangerous. It entices innocent people with deceitful promises that lead to destruction. We expose works of darkness to keep people from being caught up in them and to rescue those who already are.

Today, or one day soon, you will encounter darkness. You may even be enticed by it yourself. Make up your mind now, ahead of time, to deny the evil invitation, regardless of how attractive or enticing it is.

Never let darkness penetrate your Day One.

Never.

Flee!

Flee from sexual immorality.
1 Corinthians 6:18

Sexual temptations have always been around. When you read about the Corinthian church, you find that they lived in the midst of sexual immorality. Unfortunately, we do too. Sexual imagery is everywhere: TV, billboards, movies, books, magazines...avoiding temptation is difficult!

But temptation itself isn't sin. Acting on the temptation is sin. So how is a person to stand strong in the midst of our sex-saturated society?

Begin by realizing that sex itself is not evil. God invented sex. But He also preserved sex (and us) by making it one of the delights we share with only one other person on earth—our husband or wife. Since sex is the ultimate act of affection two people can share, it's a shame when a person has shared that sacred experience with several others before settling down with a mate. They can never fully recover that innocence they once had. Their sexual union with their spouse can never be *un*shared with previous partners.

Face it, your Day One may include a sexual temptation of some kind. Perhaps even just a mental image that you entertain for too long, knowing it's wrong to do so.

Paul's remedy is to flee sexual immorality. That means don't toy with evil imaginations. Don't go where you know you will be tempted. If porn is a problem, get accountability software. Do whatever is necessary to flee this temptation. If you don't, you may eventually become enslaved to sexual thoughts and acts. God wants more for you than that.

A Daily Dose of Humility

Humble yourselves before the Lord, and he will lift you up.

JAMES 4:10 NIV

Early in my music career, there were many humiliating experiences I would rather forget. Like concerts at Barnes & Noble that only my parents attended. Cross-country trips in a Honda Civic to play at a community college. I still have scars from tater tots thrown at my head!

Here's one of my most humiliating moments. I had just finished singing at a nearby venue and had gone across the street to a coffee shop. While I was waiting for my order, I noticed a tableful of teenagers giggling, pointing in my direction, and whispering, "I think that's him!"

My chest began to puff out as I thought to myself, *I've got my first fans. Maybe I should go sign some autographs for them.* Trying to play it cool, I casually reached for my coffee cup. Then as I turned to greet my "fans," the cup slipped out of my hands, and the entire thing spilled down the front of my jeans. I was forced to turn and face my adoring fans looking like a grown man who had just wet his pants.

Perhaps you can relate to that feeling of embarrassment. Well, I've learned that there's great value in these doses of humility. After all, if we believe everything happens for a reason, then there's something to be learned even from experiences that bruise our ego.

Let's let life's embarrassing moments guide us to a life lived with humility and remind us that it's not about us. God chooses to lift up those who humble themselves.

Day Three = Day One

I am the resurrection and the life. Whoever believes in me, though he die, yet shall he live, and everyone who lives and believes in me shall never die. Do you believe this?

John 11:25-26

On Day One, hearts were broken. Disciples were scattered. An innocent man was beaten beyond recognition and forced to carry His cross to His own death.

On Day One, evil was winning. They hurled insults at Him and mocked Him with a crown of thorns.

On Day One, He was hung on a cross between two thieves to die a slow and painful death.

Day One seemed like the end as Jesus uttered, "It is finished."

But this was not the end of the story. This was only Day One.

On day three, mourning turned to rejoicing. Death was conquered. The stone was rolled away. Scripture was fulfilled.

On day three, the sting of a Savior's crucifixion was replaced with a promise perfected. An empty tomb filled empty hearts.

On day three, Satan's plan was thwarted as the angel proclaimed, "He is risen."

Day three rewrote the death sentence Jesus was given on Day One. Day three is the reason we can celebrate Day One every day of our lives.

Today, take some time to give thanks for the death and resurrection of Jesus. He died to give you new life. He gave His life so you can step into your Day One with new mercy.

Today Is DAY ONE

World Changers

Do not neglect to do good and to share what you have, for such sacrifices are pleasing to God.

HEBREWS 13:16

Alyssa is a beautiful 13-year-old girl who is fighting for her life in a hospital in Houston. I heard her story when her parents brought her to one of my concerts. They later wrote me, telling me just how special their little girl is. Alyssa was diagnosed with a rare brain cancer, and her outlook has been less than promising. The Make-A-Wish Foundation came to her and told her to make a wish. I was blown away by her response.

Alyssa's favorite song of mine is called "Do Something." She told her parents that she felt that she was supposed to do something with her wish. She had learned in school about children in other parts of the world who lack access to clean water, so she asked Make-A-Wish to give her wish to Zimbabwe's Children by building a well for them.

Today, a well in Zimbabwe is providing clean water for children in need. Today, a 13-year-old girl in a Houston hospital room is smiling because she knows how good it feels to make a difference.

I tell you this story because Alyssa inspired me to think about how I'm living, and I hope it will do the same for you. Here's a girl who looked beyond her own circumstances and focused the needs of others.

Unbelievable! Everyone who knows Alyssa agrees that she is a true world changer. And guess what? You can be a world changer too. Dare to look beyond your own circumstances today. As you lift your eyes, God will show you ways to make a Day One kind of difference in someone else's life.

Say Goodbye to the List

Lord, if you kept a record of our sins,
who, O Lord, could ever survive?
But you offer forgiveness,
that we might learn to fear you.

Psalm 130:3-4 NLT

What is the biggest mistake you've ever made? My guess is you're scrolling through the story of your life to come up with a top-five list of wrong turns.

I know this is the case with me. I can't remember what I had for breakfast this morning, but I could tell you about choices I made ten years ago that I wish I had done differently.

It's next to impossible for us to completely forget our sins. Part of the reason is that the accuser, Satan (Revelation 12:10), is constantly trying to discourage us and fool us into believing God couldn't love someone like us. So we tend to keep a running tally of our mistakes, and the list only grows longer with time. The enemy is actively at work on our memory, making sure we not only remember, but actually relive the moments we most regret.

Here is a life-changing truth worth remembering today and every day: God has seen every choice you have made. Nothing is hidden from Him. If He wanted to, He could keep a detailed list of your sins. But instead He chooses to offer you forgiveness. He chooses to remember your sins no more (Hebrews 8:12). God's love has torn your list of sins into a million little pieces. Follow His example today and let it go!

DAY ONE

The Little Things Are the Big Things

A poor widow came and dropped in two small coins. Jesus called his disciples to him and said, "I tell you the truth, this poor widow has given more than all the others who are making contributions. For they gave a tiny part of their surplus, but she, poor as she is, has given everything she had to live on.

MARK 12:42-44 NLT

Too many times we get fooled into thinking that if we're not doing something big for God, we must not be doing enough. This attitude is so discouraging that it can leave you thinking, *I might as well not do anything at all.* But often, the good works that God has prepared for us to do *are* the little things. Ever heard the expression "Go big or go home"? Well, it may apply when talking about the importance of taking chances, but when it comes to living a life of compassion for the world around you, that expression won't fly.

When you step out in faith and obedience to do the little things God places in your path, you discover that the little things are big things in God's kingdom. Jesus illustrated this in His teaching about the poor widow who gave two small coins.

God has prepared good works for you to do today. Some may be big, and some might not be so big in your eyes. But on your way to the big thing you think you're supposed to do, don't overlook the little things you can do to show the world His love.

Today Is **DAY ONE**

When the Rest of the World Moves On

The LORD is close to the brokenhearted
and saves those who are crushed in spirit.

PSALM 34:18 NIV

I met a woman who shared with me her grief over the tragic loss of her son several months earlier. She said she felt the love and support of friends and family surrounding her at first. But as time passed, she felt people beginning to distance themselves from her because she was still having a hard time moving on with her life. They seemed to expect her to get over it quicker than she was able to.

Grief and heartbreak have no timetable. But even our closest and most trusted friends and family have a limited capacity to walk with us when our weakest moments turn into hours, days, and weeks. When the rest of the world moves on and you're still hurting, remember that God, your Comforter, is with you. He is close to you and will save you when you are "crushed in spirit." He will stay long after the hurting subsides and will walk with you through every peak and valley along the way.

I love these words to the old hymn "In the Garden."

> And He walks with me, and he talks with me,
> And he tells me I am his own;
> And the joy we share as we tarry there,
> None other has ever known.

Rest in His presence today. Rest in knowing that He will never leave you to handle heartbreak alone.

Just a Few More Days

Concerning that day or that hour, no one knows,
not even the angels in heaven, nor the
Son, but only the Father.

Mark 13:32

It doesn't take more than a few minutes of watching the news or reading the newspaper headlines before I find myself discouraged by the broken world in which we live.

Terrorist attacks, political division, economic crises, murders, natural disasters...and the list goes on.

With every senseless act of violence and every devastating storm, I find myself wondering when Jesus is coming back.

I find myself longing for that day more than ever. I think about heaven and the promise of no more pain and no more sorrow. What once was broken will be made whole. I so look forward to that day coming.

But when will it come? The Bible tells us no one knows the day or the hour. It also says God is not confined to our concept of time. "With the Lord a day is like a thousand years and a thousand years are like a day" (2 Peter 3:8 NIV). Let this Scripture fill your heart with anticipation that the day is coming. Let it also remind you that only God knows when our time will come to be called home. Let's live each day as if it's our last day on earth and the eve of our homecoming. A thousand years could be today.

God's View

Just as the heavens are higher than the earth,
so my ways are higher than your ways
and my thoughts higher than your thoughts.

ISAIAH 55:9 NLT

'm on an early morning flight to the West Coast as the sun is rising over the snowcapped mountains of Northern California. The word *beautiful* doesn't do justice to their majesty. Through a light, early morning haze, the sky is gathering its colors, and the earth is waking up. The growing light of dawn reveals a river running between two hills, winding farther than my eyes are able to follow. I can see valleys and peaks, earth and sky.

Because of my frequent travel, I have the opportunity to experience this bird's-eye view more often than most people—a chance to witness the world from high above it all. But the plane eventually has to land, bringing me back down to earth (literally and figuratively).

On an ordinary day, my feet are on the ground. I look up and see an endless sky that stretches beyond my imagination. I see mountains that look a whole lot bigger than they do from an airplane window.

The vast difference in points of view reminds me of how our lives must look to God. When all you see is a cancer diagnosis, God may see the nurse who will come to faith in Christ because of your faith during your battle. When all you see is your financial debt, God may see the miraculous way He plans to provide for you. When you see the pain of your past, God sees the healing in your future.

Remember today that God's ways are higher than yours.

Today Is

DAY ONE

Go and Sin No More

Jesus stood up again and said to the woman, "Where are your accusers? Didn't even one of them condemn you?" "No Lord," she said. And Jesus said, "Neither do I. Go and sin no more."

JOHN 8:10-11 NLT

It had all the makings of a bad day. Actually, it had all the makings of being her last day. She was publicly shamed and called out for her infidelity. The Pharisees and teachers of the Law shamelessly used her to set a trap for Jesus.

They reminded Jesus that according to the Law, this woman should be stoned to death. Jesus's response to their test quieted the crowd and turned what would have been this woman's last day into a beautiful Day One. "Let any one of you who is without sin be the first to throw a stone at her" (John 8:7 NIV).

At once, the crowd had no choice but to turn their attention away from this woman's imperfections and toward their own failings.

As for Jesus, He turned his attention toward a woman in desperate need of relief from the shame she was under. "Where are your accusers? Didn't even one of them condemn you?" "No Lord," she said. And Jesus said, "Neither do I. Go and sin no more."

When the crowd of voices in your head tries to shame you for the wrong you've done, remember this picture of Jesus and know that you are loved by a Savior who quiets the crowd and refuses to condemn the sinner. "Go and sin no more."

Today Is DAY ONE

What Are You Waiting For?

I watch in hope for the LORD,
I wait for God my Savior;
my God will hear me.

MICAH 7:7 NIV

My daughter Delaney recently reached a huge milestone in her life. She lost her first tooth. When she first realized she had a wiggly tooth, she proceeded to work that thing loose for the next six hours until at last she ran into the kitchen, holding her trophy high.

As the rest of the family ran up to congratulate her, Delaney said with a big, toothless grin, "I waited my whole life for dis!"

What are you waiting for in your life? Do you feel as if you've been waiting your whole life to see an answer to your prayer? At any given point in our lives, we might find ourselves in need of a breakthrough and wondering if our faith is strong enough to wait for God to come through.

But just as Delaney's tooth finally came out—after an entire six-year lifetime of waiting—so too will God's plan for you come at just the right time. Pray, watch, and wait. (And it's okay to jiggle the tooth once in a while.)

Make Your Now Live Forever

I am the living bread that came down from heaven.
If anyone eats of this bread, he will live forever.

JOHN 6:51

I saw a beer commercial depicting a group of young people having a poolside party as a voice invited viewers, "Make this weekend live forever." The message was that this beer offers a weekend you'll never forget.

So many messages the world sends these days sound good but are filled with empty promises. Messages like YOLO (you only live once) resonate with us because deep down we want to make the most of our lives. YOLO is a half-truth. You do only live once, but you can make sure your life lasts longer than the here and now, and not by buying a certain beer. It's by partaking of the "living bread that came down from heaven."

I spoke with a man who said he felt a stirring to make the most of his life. With a hugely successful career in the business world, he appears to personify the American dream. But he told me that the corporate world is all about the here and now. He said something that struck me in a profound way: "I don't want to live for now. I want to live forever."

The world's definition of the good life can't begin to compare to God's offer of eternal life. We make the most of our time not by living *for* this moment, but by living *in* this moment, ever mindful of eternity.

Ask God to give you a greater hunger for His living bread, leaving no appetite for the empty promises of this world. You only live once, but with God's help you can live your now in such a way that it echoes for eternity.

Today Is DAY ONE

He Will Answer You

Call to me and I will answer you and tell you
great and unsearchable things you do not know.
JEREMIAH 33:3 NIV

A recurring theme running throughout this book is also a recurring theme throughout Scripture—the call to prayer. And every instruction Scripture gives to pray is connected with a wonderful promise: When you pray, God will hear you and answer you. Jeremiah 33:3 invites us to pray and reminds us what the effect will be—"Call to me and I will answer you."

God is telling you that He is not absent. He is not far off. He is not distracted. He is present. He will not ignore you when you come to Him. He's listening for you and waiting for you to call on Him.

And when you call on Him, He will answer you. What's more, the Scripture goes on to say He will "tell you great and unsearchable things you do not know." The word *unsearchable* points to something that is beyond understanding.

Riches of wisdom wait for you when you choose to call out to God. God is ready to teach you and show you things beyond anything you can learn from anyone or anything else.

Spend time in His presence today. Call to Him with great anticipation of receiving not only the answers to your prayers but also "great and unsearchable things."

Grace Wins

Sin is no longer your master, for you no longer
live under the requirements of the law. Instead,
you live under the freedom of God's grace.

ROMANS 6:14 NLT

A life in Christ is a victorious life. So why do we spend so many of our days drowning in defeat?

I wonder if you can relate to this: In my most discouraging moments, I imagine God shaking His head in disgrace, disappointment written all over His face as if He were saying, "Matthew, why can't you ever get it right?"

In my weakest moments, the guilt I feel for my sin makes me believe that God's grace won't reach far enough to save me this time. These destructive thoughts can steal my joy.

But as this book's title says, today is Day One. A chance to choose to reject the lies of the enemy, who's doing everything he can to keep us knocked down and out by guilt and shame.

But Satan's power is no match for God's grace. "Sin is no longer your master." It's important to recognize the battle that's going on for our soul every single day. It's very real, this tug-of-war inside us. But make no mistake—we've been promised victory! God has not given up on me or you, and He never will. In the war between guilt and grace, God's will for you is to be living proof that His grace wins every time.

Day One for the Prodigal Son

The father said to his servants, "Bring the fattened calf and kill it. Let's have a feast and celebrate. For this son of mine was dead and is alive again; he was lost and is found."

LUKE 15:22-24 NIV

In his mind, the day the prodigal son left home was his Day One. He was no longer under Dad's roof and no longer bound by Dad's rules. But we know how the story goes from here. He burned through his inheritance, hit rock bottom, and longed for the home he had been in such a hurry to leave.

We can all relate to that son's decision to go his own way. This is a daily struggle in me—and probably in you too. *Am I going to trust my heavenly Father's plan for me today, or do I know what's best?* I may not always stop and literally ask myself that question, but I do answer the question by the way I rush headfirst into my will and ignore God's best plan for my life.

But this story isn't just about the rebellion of the prodigal son. This is a story about the *return* of the prodigal son, who came crawling back, humbled and asking for a job as one of his father's servants.

Upon his return, the son wasn't forced to work his way back into the family. He wasn't told he would have to start at the bottom. No, he was welcomed back with open arms as his father came running out to greet him. His return was celebrated with a feast! The prodigal son discovered that true freedom was found in his return to the one who loved him most.

This is where our true freedom is found as well. Have you chosen your own way over God's plan lately? Return to your heavenly Father, who loves you deeply. He not only welcomes you with open arms, He celebrates your return.

Renewed Day by Day

So we do not lose heart. Though our outer self is wasting away, our inner self is being renewed day by day.

2 CORINTHIANS 4:16

After driving the same truck for 12 years, I recently broke down and bought a new car. My truck was big, and it had a huge gas tank. The downside? One trip to the gas station cost more than my mortgage. The upside? It seemed like I could go weeks between fill-ups.

This time I bought a smaller vehicle, and I'm visiting the gas station more often than I used to. Seems as if every time I look at the fuel gauge, it's on empty and I'm in need of a pit stop.

Now, I know this sounds crazy, but God has a way of showing me things about my relationship with Him at the strangest times. A recent gas station visit was the scene this time. Standing at the gas pump, my thoughts turned to a comparison of my spiritual life with that big old truck I used to own. I settle for the occasional quiet time with God or a church service on a Sunday as if that will fill me up and last me for days or even weeks before I'm on empty again and in need of spiritual nourishment.

God offers us a day-by-day fill-up of His love, wisdom, strength, and grace. So why would we settle for just an occasional spiritual boost? Ask God to bring your heart back to Him daily. Walk with Him every day, not just every now and then. And know that God is not a God who renews you once in a while, but day by day.

A Self-Guided Tour

This God is our God for ever and ever.
He will be our guide even to the end.
PSALM 48:14 NIV

Have you ever opted for the self-guided tour at a museum or historical site instead of following a knowledgeable tour guide? I made the mistake of doing this once, and I won't make it again. My wife and I had traveled to Florence, Italy, a city rich with history and incredible art museums. We were young and traveling on a budget, so we decided just to get a map and make our own way through the city instead of spending the extra money on a legitimate tour guide. It wasn't until after I returned to the States and a friend began asking me if I visited this museum or saw that famous sculpture that I began to realize how much I missed by trying to navigate the trip by myself.

I do the same thing in my spiritual life, foolishly opting for the self-guided tour instead of seeking God's guidance. And as I missed so many sights in Italy, every time I walk through my day without seeking God's guidance, I miss opportunities to experience all that He wants to show me.

Remember this today: The One who knows every detail of your life will lead you on the most fulfilling path for your life. Don't settle for a self-guided tour today. Follow Him, knowing that "He will be our guide even to the end."

Weeds

Consider the lilies, how they grow: they neither toil nor spin, yet I tell you, even Solomon in all his glory was not arrayed like one of these.

LUKE 12:27

"**D**addy, look! Pretty flowers!"

I turned to my little three-year-old girl to see what beautiful display of botany she had discovered during our neighborhood walk. I expected to find her pointing to a red rosebush, maybe some yellow daisies, or even a patch of wildflowers. Instead, she was pointing to some gangly-looking weeds she had proudly picked for me to see.

My first instinct was to say, "Oh no, honey, those aren't flowers; those are just weeds." You know, educate her on the reality that those weeds will never qualify for the favorable distinction of being in the flower family. But instead, I saved the flower lesson for another day, and together we marveled at the wonder of the weeds.

My daughter taught me something about God that day. We might look at someone and have a tendency to place him or her in the category of a weed. We might see the ex-convict, the bully, the alcoholic, the homeless, the troubled...and wonder how God could use them.

But when we see weeds, God sees something beautiful in the making. Just like my daughter on our walk that day, God marvels at the wonder of the weeds. And we can marvel at the wonder of how He turns weeds into beautiful things. Ask God to help you see the beauty in the weeds as you walk through the world today.

Today Is DAY ONE

Can't Get Any Worse

Listen to my cry, for I am in desperate need.
PSALM 142:6 NIV

Ever have one of those days when you find yourself thinking, *Surely, it can't get any worse*, and then it does? Today was one of those days for me.

The setting—Atlanta airport. The villain—a certain airline that shall remain nameless. First one delay and then another and another until my flight to Asheville was finally canceled altogether. There was no way I was going to make my scheduled performance. And this wasn't just any performance. This was a special invite from a very important retailer who had promised to help my new record and my career. This was a big deal.

Standing in the long line of people waiting to be rerouted, the reality began to sink in that I had spent all day in this lousy airport only to fly right back home.

A nice lady at the help desk said, "I'm sorry for your delay."

I smiled and responded, "Your airline hurt my career today."

Once again, she apologized. But as I walked away, I realized what a foolish statement I had made. That statement was evidence of my lack of trust that God was in control. I was trapped in this headspace, thinking God would allow an airline to determine the course of my career. As if God were less powerful than an airline.

We serve a God who knows everything and has our best interests at heart. A God who is always at work, orchestrating even the smallest details of our lives. Rest in knowing that while you may be caught off guard by your circumstances, God is not surprised, and His plan is still very much intact.

All the Days of My Life

One thing I ask from the Lord, this only do I seek: that I may dwell in the house of the Lord all the days of my life.

Psalm 27:4

So now what? You've reached the final chapter of this little Day One book, but the sun is going to rise tomorrow, and there are more days to come for you. How will you choose to go about the rest of your days in this life? My hope in writing both the song "Day One" and this book was to encourage a shift in thinking that might spark a fire in your heart to make the most of the days God blesses you with.

This is my prayer for you: May you wake up each morning and be reminded with the rising of the sun that God's mercy is new, and you are free to live a life not defeated by sin, but victorious by grace.

When you feel the gravitational pull of this broken world to simply settle for a mundane life, may you listen to the stirring in your soul that cries out for more than the status quo, and may you reach for life to the fullest.

When you're tempted to look back at the past and relive the defeat of yesterday's sins, may you fight off the lies of the enemy and hold tightly to the promise that you are a new creation. May you face each Day One knowing you don't have to face it alone, remembering that your Savior walks with you and will guide your steps along the way. And may you take time each day to have your strength renewed in the presence of God, praying and reading Scripture.

Finally, my prayer for you is that when your final Day One on this earth has ended, you will hear your heavenly Father say, "Well done," and you will be welcomed into eternity to dwell in the house of the Lord all the Day Ones of your eternal life.

Matthew West is a multiple ASCAP Christian Music Songwriter/Artist of the Year winner, a four-time GRAMMY nominee, and an American Music Award and Billboard Music Award winner. His songwriting credits include cuts by Rascal Flatts, Billy Ray Cyrus, Diamond Rio, and more. His song "Hello, My Name Is" topped the Billboard Singles Chart for a record 17 weeks. A consummate storyteller, Matthew has collected more than 40,000 personal stories from across the globe, inspiring many of his hit songs. Matthew and his family make their home in Tennessee.

Be sure to enjoy Matthew's other fine books
from Harvest House Publishers...

When Grammy-nominated recording artist Matthew West started writing his top-selling album *The Story of Your Life*, he asked fans to submit personal experiences. More than 10,000 tales of hope, perseverance, and redemption poured in. With friend and author Angela Thomas, Matthew presents some of these powerful stories paired with meaningful devotions they inspired.

- Wendy gave birth to her daughter in jail. When all seemed hopeless, she found God, and her life transformed into something beautiful.

- Cory, a married youth pastor, had an affair, and his life fell apart. With God's mercy, he and his wife gathered the broken pieces and started again.

- Sheila always struggled with severe insecurity. Now she lives confidently in the purpose God has for her.

This unforgettable devotional journey will inspire you to discover God as the author of your unique life and to share the power of your story. Also available—a companion DVD of the same title and a stand-alone guide, *The Story of Your Life Interactive Journey.* The DVD and book help you, individually or as part of a group study, personalize and explore more deeply the messages of God's hope and redemption in your own story.

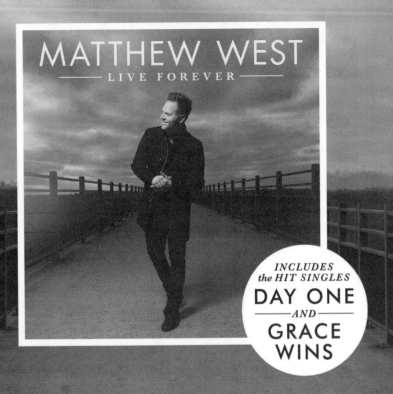

MATTHEW WEST
— LIVE FOREVER —

INCLUDES
the HIT SINGLES
DAY ONE
—AND—
GRACE WINS

ALSO AVAILABLE
INTO THE LIGHT

FEATURING
HELLO, MY NAME IS +
FORGIVENESS + DO SOMETHING

To learn more about *Live Forever* and the stories behind the songs visit
www.matthewwest.com

To learn more about Harvest House books and
to read sample chapters, visit our website:

www.harvesthousepublishers.com

HARVEST HOUSE PUBLISHERS
EUGENE, OREGON